Ruby

Commonsense Design

Commonsense Design/ A COMPLETE GUIDE TO GOOD INTERIOR DESIGN ON A BUDGET

by ARNOLD FRIEDMANN

Illustrations and Collaboration by
PHILIP F. FARRELL, JR.

CHARLES SCRIBNER'S SONS/NEW YORK

Text copyright © 1976 Arnold Friedmann
Illustrations copyright © 1976 Philip F. Farrell, Jr.

Library of Congress Cataloging in Publication Data
Friedmann, Arnold.
    Commonsense design.
    1. House furnishings.   2. Interior decoration.
I. Farrell, Philip F.   II. Title.
TX311.F74   747'.8'831   76-15179
ISBN 0-684-14685-1
ISBN 0-684-14688-6 pbk.

CONTENTS

PART THREE

Commonsense Design

Introduction

This is a book about good design. Its purpose is to help you solve design problems in your house or apartment for the least possible amount of money.

The desire to create a pleasant, functional, and livable environment is one of the basic human needs. Although interior design as a profession is relatively new, man's concern with shelter and the improvement of his surroundings dates back to earliest history; the decoration of caves predates even the simplest form of man-made structures. Throughout the history of art and architecture, interiors have assumed as much importance as exteriors, and it is surprising that the professional activity in this field did not begin until the early decades of this century. Historically, interiors were created by architects, artists, and laymen, and the term *interior decorator*, denoting a "professional," emerged only around 1930 in the United States. There is nothing wrong with that phrase; it is still widely used. However, because so many amateurs—curtain makers, upholsterers, painters—refer to themselves as interior decorators, most serious professionals prefer to call themselves *interior designers*.

Professional interior designers usually have at least four years of art school or college education; they study planning, design, architectural details, and history and acquire a thorough professional education. In order to become a competent designer, however, it is not enough to be trained exclusively in residential design and decoration. Interior designers must also know how to deal with *any* kind of interior space—large or small, public or private. And they must learn much about the environment in general, from design principles to architecture, and from art to lighting and mechanical equipment. Many designers work in large firms or architectural offices, where they deal with public buildings, stores, restaurants, offices, and hotels; others prefer residential interior design and often work independently or in small firms. Professional designers do more than select furniture, fabrics, and colors. Their services include space analysis, programming, design, planning, detailing, supervision of construction, as well as the coordination of lighting and mechanical equipment and the selection and specification of all furnishings.

The major professional society for interior designers is called the ASID (American Society of Interior Designers); the major society for architects is the AIA (American Institute of Architects). Membership in these organizations does not guarantee great design, but it does imply that members have met professional standards as set by these societies. A national design examination and professional knowledge is now a prerequisite for membership in the ASID. (Many stores offer some kind of design service to their customers; make sure it is an accredited designer you are listening to and not a salesperson whose job is to sell you something.)

Since the emphasis in this book is on budget design, my recommendations are for relatively simple interiors of apartments and houses. But a basic guide can be helpful in any circumstances, and that is what this book is all about.

It takes experience and learning to master all the basic principles of design. Making the right decisions within the limitations of a budget is even more of a challenge. In addition, we live in a society abounding in choices—good and bad, cheap and expensive. The expense of many products does not necessarily indicate the quality of their design. To distinguish between good and bad requires some understanding and self-confidence.

The beautiful interiors illustrated in many popular magazines are expensive and professionally designed. The same is often true of exhibitions and model rooms. Not only was a budget not a serious consideration there, but what often looks exciting in a razzle-dazzle show-biz context might be difficult to live with. Many handsome books feature elegant homes with interiors that would be expensive to re-create.

Fortunately, good design does not have a price tag. Many interiors created on a very limited budget are more imaginative and appropriate than some very costly installations. A little guidance is all that is necessary.

The key to good interior design is a truly personal environment. For instance, no matter how beautifully a hotel room might have been designed, it will, quite obviously, always lack the personality of its occupant. No matter how exciting a model room might appear, it remains just that—a room in a furniture or department store. Spaces that have been designed or assembled "correctly," or according to some sound design principles, are not necessarily appealing or inviting; and spaces that have been put together as highly personal expressions will not necessarily succeed as good design. The proper balance between functional considerations and personal expression is the aim—one that does not necessarily require a lot of money.

Several basic design principles can be understood fairly easily; they are discussed in the first chapter. Some have to do with the dimensions of space and the size of individual pieces of furniture. One must understand scale relationships, form, and texture. It is important to know something about materials—their qualities and maintenance requirements. And it is important to understand a little about the way furnishings are built.

There are situations, of course, where the guidance and services of a professional will be well worth the expense. If you have to design a kitchen from scratch, for example, or if you are considering structural alterations, you should obtain at least some basic expert advice. There are a number of professionals, both interior designers and architects, who offer their consulting services on an hourly basis. The investment is usually worthwhile.

The general information in this book, together with some of the specific suggestions and hints, should take you a long way toward making the right decisions on your own. If you follow the suggested planning process before buying furnishings, creating a well-designed, inexpensive home should be easy and enjoyable.

PART ONE

1/Good Design

Good design refers to qualities above and beyond those which are merely fashionable at a particular time and place. Perhaps the only area of total agreement about what is beautiful can be found in nature. Most of us would agree about beautiful trees, about rock formations, and about landscape. Nature seems never to "design" anything in a capricious fashion; the natural shapes of plants and animals usually serve a purpose or function. In attempting to evaluate what man has created, it is helpful to consider some of the criteria so very apparent in our natural surroundings. Frequently, man-made objects designed for a strictly functional purpose are very beautiful, even though the creators were not designers and gave no conscious thought to the visual qualities of their designs. From primitive tools to sophisticated optical equipment, from early foot bridges to twentieth-century suspension bridges, and from simple rough-hewn furniture to an "engineered" tractor seat, we find examples of great beauty without the benefit of planned aesthetic design.

I do not mean that good design is purely a matter of purpose and function. The famous dictum "Form follows function" is by no means enough to understand and evaluate the qualities of design. It is, however, an important and helpful criterion to keep in mind. Some people have tried to define beauty as "truth" or "honesty," and again these would be overly simplistic criteria for evaluation. But there is merit indeed in an honest use of material and in an honest expression of function whether in a building or in an object.

Well-designed chairs and tables of plastic used in an appropriate and expressive way.

16/COMMONSENSE DESIGN

At the beginning of the Industrial Revolution, many products were made to imitate handmade things. The first automobiles were literal imitations of horse-drawn carriages and were known as horseless carriages. Even today, especially in home furnishings, there is an overabundance of silly imitations. For instance, plastic products are still relatively new, and for that reason many manufacturers are reluctant to use the material in its own honest and beautiful way. Plastic happens to lend itself to almost any form, shape, and color—so everything from stones to brick to wood is copied in plastic! Only in recent years have plastics found acceptance in some well-designed, elegant, honestly expressive forms: in chairs and furnishings, in dishes, and in a whole variety of household products. The designers have created more than a purely functional expression; they have created a beautiful and appropriate form.

American society is probably the most future-oriented of all the industrialized nations. We believe in new inventions, in gadgets, and in progressive ideas. We may have to modify our attitudes somewhat with the shortage of natural resources and energy supplies, but this will probably not shake our firm belief in the merits of new over old and today over yesterday. This belief is seen in our buildings, our appliances, our kitchens and household equipment, in our offices and industrial equipment, and certainly in our automobiles. Strangely enough, the exact opposite is true in our attitudes toward furniture and interior design. For some reason we have established a value system whereby a young couple may equip their first apartment with simple modern furnishings, but as they progress in age and income they feel they should be surrounded by "traditional" furnishings.

Of course the styles and periods from each era have influenced succeeding eras. Indeed, almost anything that is designed today has some roots in history. Many magnificent examples of period furnishings and period rooms have survived and can be seen today in museums and stately homes. Most of the English and French styles that we admire date back no further than the eighteenth century; our own American tradition was basically an interpretation of the contemporary popular furniture in England. Our most *original* furniture was that fashioned by craftsmen and pioneers, from the woods at hand and with simple tools, for maximum function and efficiency—in particular, furniture reflecting the philosophy and life-styles of religious groups such as the Shakers.

A most fascinating aspect of period furniture and historic interiors is the

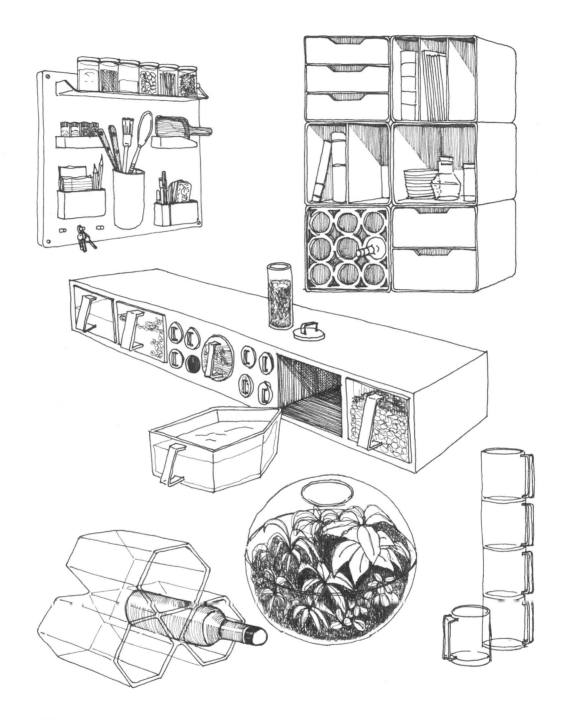

Plastic products can be well designed, even elegant.

relationship of fashion and design to the social, cultural, and technological mores of a particular period. If early American furniture reflects the pioneering spirit of the early settlers, Louis XVth furniture reflects the life at court, the somewhat frivolous activities of the nobility of that time, the clothes, the music, and even the style of dance. Chippendale or Sheraton furniture mirrors the somewhat more sedate mores of eighteenth-century England. The size and scale of these furnishings also relate to the size and scale of the homes for which they were created; often antiques or accurate reproductions from such periods can hardly fit into the kinds of spaces we live in today. The craftsmen at the time were creating things in keeping with the contemporary life-style, but they were also trying to produce furnishings as advanced in design and technology as the tools at their disposal permitted.

Rich and mighty American tycoons in the late nineteenth and early twentieth centuries had the means to buy some European palaces and estates and have them rebuilt here, or to have the interiors refitted into similarly scaled American mansions. It is in part because of these acquisitions by glamorous moguls that eighteenth-century European antiques are often considered the epitome of luxury and good taste.

Taste is a changing system of preferences or fashions that are common to a social group, a nation, or a period of time. When we think of "good taste" the chances are that we think of our own preferences, or those of people whom we admire. Eighteenth- and nineteenth-century American society admired the cultural achievements of Europe—the artistic, the architectural, and certainly the decorative. Manufacturers of furniture (who until recently rarely employed designers) tended rather blindly to perpetuate this preference. While we developed the fine art of copying, many other countries continued to develop new styles and designs. For instance, in a movement spearheaded at the Bauhaus (School of Design) in Germany in the 1920s and early 1930s, some beautiful pieces of furniture were designed by Mies van der Rohe, Marcel Breuer, and others which are still considered superb examples of modern design both here and in Europe.

One of the most difficult design questions concerns good reproductions and, indeed, the definition of a reproduction. If a chair was made in Chippendale's workshop, is that the only valid Chippendale chair? What about those that were made according to his designs in other shops during his lifetime; or the ones that were made after his death? These philosophical questions do not concern us much in dealing with budget interiors, but they should be kept in mind in dealing with furniture selection. Ideally, of course, the original is always the best. No matter how hard an artist or craftsman tries, a copy can rarely come up to the level of the original. The real problem today is that there are very few good period reproductions available at a reasonable price. When they are "in the style of" of "in the manner of" something else and not line-for-line, reproductions are even less successful. A twentieth-century designer or craftsman cannot really design anything that is seventeenth- or eighteenth-century, no matter how hard he tries, since he lives in the present. Many fashionable periods that are advertised or exhibited have no relationship to the original period design at all. Numerous "styles" that never existed have been invented and sold to the public, "Mediterranean Provincial," for example, which was invented by clever salesmen to capture a market enthralled by both the so-called Mediterranean and Provincial styles.

As I have mentioned, early in this century high-quality modern design developed much further in Europe than in the United States. The strong tradition of craftsmanship in the Scandinavian countries, for instance, developed and refined wooden furniture to the point of making "Scandinavian"-style furniture popular and universally accepted.

When modern furnishings as we know them today first appeared in the United States, many designs were cheap and poorly made. With the exception of a very few manufacturers who employed talented designers, the concept of modern design was associated with cheap furnishings. The resulting inexpensive "dinette sets" (lots of chrome and plastic) or the inexpensive products made for motels ("motel modern") increased the public's reluctance to accept anything but "traditional" designs.

I do not mean to discourage the use of antiques or objects of sentimental value, nor do I wish to suggest that the only kind of acceptable interior design is a strictly modern approach. It is much more important that each of us lives in an environment we enjoy and appreciate. But some basic design criteria must be recognized. In discussing the value and cost of things, it is important to understand what makes certain ones more desirable or more valuable or more beautiful. The ideal way of looking at design in general, and furnishings in particular, has little to do with history and styles. Many ancient and historic furnishings are poorly designed and ugly, but fortunately not too many of those have survived. What one should try to look for is not so much the difference between traditional and modern design as the difference between good design and bad design.

Finally, I think that in order to create good interior design two things are important: to know when to stop and to do at least one thing well. It is much easier to achieve an elegant or pleasant interior if one does not overdo things with too much furniture, too much color, too many textures, too many patterns, too many styles. All will fight for attention, with the end result being confusion. Consider some extra unfurnished space. It might be much more serene than another unnecessary object stuck into each empty spot.

And do at least one thing well rather than trying to use every possible idea and trick in each room. If a room has a wonderful view, an attractive fireplace, or some other prominent architectural feature, that might be enough to give it character. If a vibrant color scheme has been used, the color alone might carry the room. If there are some interesting pieces of furniture or decorative objects, there is no point in introducing an elaborate window treatment to compete with them. And if there is a lively pattern in a rug or upholstery or wall covering, the introduction of patterns in lots of other areas would detract from it. There is no rule that only one idea or one theme can be used in any given space, but as a general guideline it is wise—and certainly more subtle—to understate.

A famous twentieth-century architect, Ludwig Mies van der Rohe, was the originator of the saying "Less is more." That idea in architecture and in interior design can be a very helpful principle—and most certainly one that will keep the budget at a reasonable level.

2/Design Terms

Some fields of learning have developed their own language, consisting of specialized words unfamiliar to the layman. Design vocabulary contains many familiar terms; they can be confusing, since everyone attaches different meanings to them. It seems a good idea, therefore, briefly to explain what designers mean by *scale, proportion, form,* and *texture* and what these terms mean in reference to residential interiors.

SCALE

Scale has two important meanings for the designer and for anybody concerned with planning space. One meaning refers to the use of small dimensions to represent larger ones, as in drawings of plans or maps. The other meaning, to which I refer here, deals with the relationship of things to one another or to people. Objects or buildings always relate to something else. The moment a space exists, objects in it establish a scale relationship to that space and to each other.

A number of critics have questioned the height and mass of the two World Trade Center towers in New York City because of their inhuman scale. These buildings would certainly be out of place adjoining a village common. If one were to take a grand piano and place it in a room measuring 8 by 10 feet, the piano would look out of place because of its scale, no matter how beautiful an object it might be.

The spaces we live in today are quite small. Some people are fortunate enough to live in older houses or in the exceptional new building where ceiling heights might be 9 feet, 10 feet, or even more; but most ceilings in residences built in the last few decades are just about 8 feet high, and the square-foot dimensions are equally limited. However, a good deal of furniture is still being marketed which does not take these obvious facts into consideration. Breakfronts copied from eighteenth-century designs are out of scale in small twentieth-century dining areas. In fact, some old pieces and reproductions simply will not fit into contemporary homes.

We must also realize that people are the most critical determinants for all dimensions, and everything that we build and use must be in scale to human dimensions. A very deep sofa might look inviting, but if it has not been scaled properly, it will be uncomfortable. By the same token, delicate chairs might be interesting to look at but extremely difficult to sit on.

If you are assembling a variety of furnishings for a given space, keep in mind that each one relates to every other one. Let us suppose that you have acquired several pieces of furniture for your living room—one fairly bulky and several smaller. Placing all of these objects in one group, with nothing at the other side or at the end of the same space, would be out of scale and would throw the room out of balance. If, however, you place your bulky object on one side of the room and balance it with the smaller pieces on the other side, you may achieve a harmonious effect.

PROPORTION

Scale is at the same time a matter of proportion. Proportion is most often the criterion applied to relative dimensions of spaces or objects. A typical living room will be in good proportion with a ceiling height of 8 to 12 feet. A ceiling height of 40 or 50 feet would, of course, be out of proportion for that room. By the same token a public building such as a theater, which does have a very high ceiling, would be out of proportion with a ceiling of 8 feet. Furnishings and all objects that we use can have good proportions or poor ones. There are no precise formulas for good proportion, although the history of art is full of valiant attempts to establish such rules.

Artists, designers, and architects spend years studying such basic concepts as proportion, and ultimately they can create good proportions intuitively. But it is not necessary to devote years of study to design your own environment. Perhaps the most important thing is simply to be aware of these concepts, making a conscious attempt to perceive physical surroundings somewhat more critically. Proportion has much to do with function and with the proper use of materials. It is easy, for example, to recognize and understand a brick not only through its color and material but also through its proportion. If the proportions of a brick were changed substantially, it would be a totally different building block.

FORM

Form in interior design refers to individual objects or to the combination of these objects into a complete configuration. Architects or product designers often create new forms, while the interior designer combines many existing elements. In putting together a living environment, you will have to make judgments about the form of specific objects and about the overall form created from the combination of these choices.

In analyzing products or furnishings and evaluating their merits, we often use words such as *order, clarity, expressiveness, truth,* and *organization.* All these are attributes which somehow make for good or satisfying form. The following checklist deals with these qualities and can be applied to objects or buildings or furniture:

> What is it? Does it express its purpose and function?
> What is it designed to do? Does it do so well?
> Whom is it for?
> What is it made of, and is the material appropriate?
> How was it made and why? Does it make sense?
> Are the construction principles sound?
> Will it last?
> Could it be made more simply?
> Is it beautiful and is the form satisfying?
> How much does it cost?

Notice that the question of beauty is almost the last one. If all the other questions can be answered logically and affirmatively, then the object probably is well designed. Knowing for whom and for what purpose something was created will often give you a clue to the appropriateness of the price. Some very beautiful things are created as luxury objects; that does not mean that you will be unable to find equally well-designed objects for far less money.

Good form is determined by the conscious or subconscious combination of other design elements I have mentioned (scale, proportion) and also by other elements of design such as texture, pattern, unity, rhythm, and sequence.

TEXTURE AND PATTERN

Every material used in interiors has texture, but not necessarily pattern. Some textures are so minute that we cannot discern them without magnification. Textures are in every building material, too; the textural quality of buildings is a significant aspect of architecture. While the texture of a building affects us only visually, we become aware of interior textures through our sense of touch as well, and thus this element of interior design is very important. Perhaps I should repeat the dictum "Less is more" as one of the most helpful hints for the selection of textures and patterns. I do not mean that textures and patterns cannot be combined with great success, or that they should not be used extensively. In general, however, the combination of too many textures and too many patterns spells trouble.

If you really enjoy a space, whether it is a home, an office, or a public building, look at it carefully to see how many textures or materials were used. The chances are that a space to which you have responded favorably did not use a combination of many different materials. The scale of textures is particularly important, visually as well as kinetically; and smooth textures reflect light, while heavy textures absorb it. You will not be able to create a light and airy space if wall surfaces, fabrics, and floor coverings are heavily textured, even though the colors may be bright and light.

Materials that we touch can be pleasant and sensuous. The feeling of silk is lush compared to the feeling of burlap. Sandpaper feels unpleasant, and to many people certain fabrics such as fiber glass have a similarly unpleasant feel. Simple functional principles can help you decide which textures to use. For example, it is not particularly comfortable to sit on plastic materials or leather on very hot days. There is a considerable price differential between leather and vinyl plastics, but perhaps neither of these materials is ideal for hot-weather use.

Most interiors require certain textures, depending upon their use, but in spite of my warning not to overdo things, it is good principle to have more than just one material or texture in a room. A space that has wall paneling made of plastic laminate, a vinyl asbestos floor, a smooth ceiling, all plastic laminate furniture, and upholstery in vinyl plastics could perhaps be the waiting room in a bus terminal. If you have chosen a rather deeply textured pile carpet, the materials used for upholstery should probably not compete; they should instead balance the overall textural effect.

Balance is the key word for patterns as well. If you use a bold pattern in curtains, other patterns in the rooms should be smaller or more delicate in relation to the one dominant one. Alternatively, one strong pattern in a space might come off best if the other materials in the room are just woven textures and smooth fabrics. A bold or strong pattern might appear on wallpaper, on the sofa fabric, or in a rug; in each case it will then be a good idea to restrict the dominant pattern to that one area and use more subdued materials elsewhere. This is not an inviolate rule, however, for some people have the ability to combine many strong colors, patterns, and textures successfully.

I have singled out the most important concepts for interior design. Other design elements, such as unity, rhythm, and sequence, are of greater significance to architecture than to interior design. Color and light, two very important design elements, are discussed in greater detail in separate chapters.

The great importance here is that all these elements are closely interrelated. Every single design element is present in any space, even if not consciously considered. Fireplaces, large windows, high ceilings, or textured plaster walls, wooden floors, louvered closets or windows—all are examples that may exist in your space, and must be taken into account. Try to keep a kind of mental checklist and ask yourself from time to time whether you have considered all the design aspects for selecting individual items and, more importantly, for the total configuration.

3/ Planning

Planning is essential for towns, communities, and buildings. It is equally important for interior design. If you are about to start planning your own home or apartment, you will already have a large part of the program in your mind, since you have a general idea of your needs and intentions, as well as of your budget. Even if you do not perceive any special problems, a bit of planning before you rush out and start buying will be the best thing you can do to keep to a reasonable budget.

The first aspect of planning deals with function. It concerns the traffic patterns through rooms and areas: how you enter your home with bags of groceries; where you can put them down; whether you can remove your kitchen garbage conveniently; how members of your household have access to the bathroom facilities; and whether, if there are outdoor spaces involved, you have access to them. The functional aspect of planning also concerns the placement of furniture in each individual area: adequate seating; access to a dining table; access to closets; appropriate distances for conversation and for viewing television; and adequate space and access for any variety of activities that you might have in mind. The way a door swings (Does it interfere with traffic or a piece of furniture?); the height of window sills (Does furniture block part of a window or view?); whether certain activities or placements of furnishings interfere with the heating or air conditioning—all these considerations are functional aspects of planning. Each decision can and should be considered in plan form.

/27

The second aspect of planning deals with more abstract considerations of design. A plan will reveal the balance, the proportion, and the form of a particular space. If a couple of large chests are placed on each side of a sofa, and if the sofa is flanked by two heavy armchairs and on the opposite side of the room is a single delicate chair, the room will look strangely out of balance. Visual shortcomings of this sort immediately become apparent if one works from a plan.

It is quite easy to draw a plan. The short time it takes to make one can save a great deal of money and work. It is much faster and easier to push furniture around on paper than on Saturday afternoon! If you make a mistake on paper, it can be corrected in two seconds by erasing it. If you make a mistake in real life you may have to live with it for a long time. Let us suppose you want to purchase a sofa, some tables, and perhaps some shelving to be placed on a certain wall; a plan will tell you exactly how large these pieces can be. Something that looks just right in the showroom might turn out to be 2 or 3 inches too long. If a plan is drawn to scale, you can easily see whether a room will be overcrowded, whether you will have easy access to your dining table or a closet, and so on. A scale plan is perhaps the most important professional tool for interior design, and since it is so simple to do there is no reason why you cannot use this approach yourself.

The most common scale used for interior and architectural plans is 1/4 inch = 1 foot. You do not need an architectural scale ruler. You can use any ruler, such as a carpenter's folding ruler (very handy to measure your space in the first place). Remember that every 1/4 inch on the ruler represents 1 foot in real life. Almost any stationery store sells graph paper, and the kind that you should buy will be divided into 1/4-inch grid spaces. The first thing to do is measure your rooms and carefully draw a plan of the existing spaces. To avoid mistakes, record the dimensions the way designers and architects do, by writing dimensions in feet and inches. Thus a wall will be 12 feet 2 inches long, rather than 146 inches long. By making a quick and approximate freehand plan of the shape of the space first, you can write in all these dimensions as you measure, before transposing them to your finished plan on graph paper. Be sure to measure door openings, windows, and any other architectural features of the room such as radiators, closets, closet doors, elaborate moldings, and projecting columns. Once the outline has been drawn as

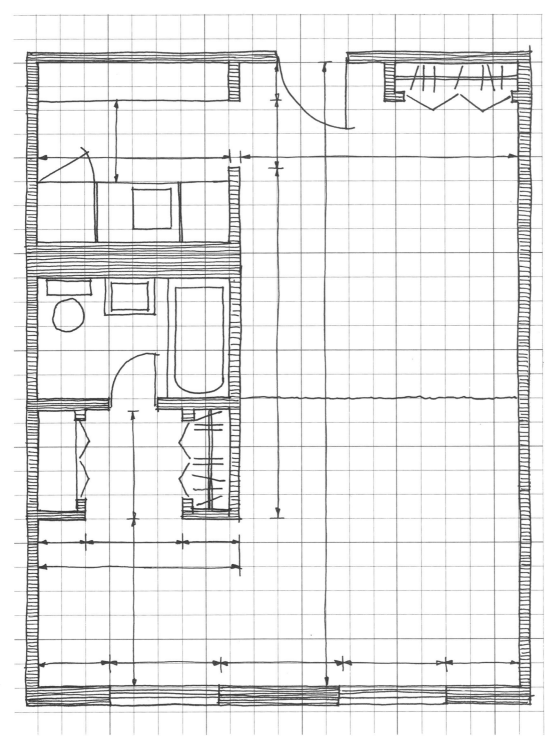

An example of a plan drawn to scale, showing key architectural features and dimension lines. 1/4" = 1'.

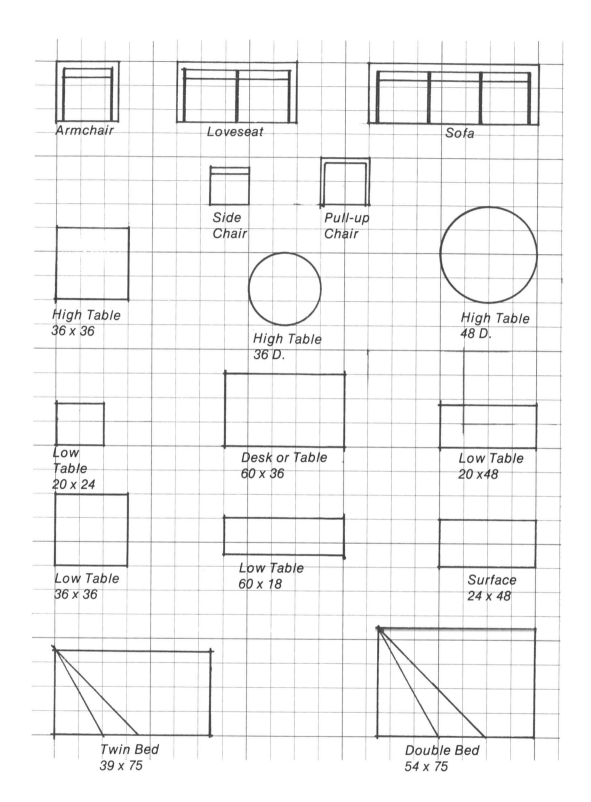

Armchair

Loveseat

Sofa

Side Chair

Pull-up Chair

High Table
36 x 36

High Table
36 D.

High Table
48 D.

Low Table
20 x 24

Desk or Table
60 x 36

Low Table
20 x 48

Low Table
36 x 36

Low Table
60 x 18

Surface
24 x 48

Twin Bed
39 x 75

Double Bed
54 x 75

Examples of typical furniture symbols drawn to scale. 1/4" = 1'.

accurately as possible on graph paper, it will probably be useful to go over it with a rather heavy pencil line.

You are now ready to begin planning furniture. Page 30 shows some typical pieces of furniture, all drawn in 1/4-inch scale. These drawings are plan symbols, and they do not necessarily indicate the exact shape of the particular chair, table, or sofa that you have in mind. If the size is more or less correct, the symbol will do. If you are considering an armchair which is much larger than the 30 x 32-inch dimension shown here, it will be important to make that adjustment. If your sofa is 8 feet long instead of 6 1/2 feet like the one shown here, you must be sure to make that adjustment, too. Measure your own armchair or sofa and draw it to scale.

You can trace the furniture symbols you need and transfer them with carbon paper onto fairly heavy paper or light cardboard. If you cut out these shapes carefully, you will have a set of templates that enables you to move furniture around on your plan until you find the most satisfactory arrangement. Or you can use thin tracing paper or onionskin as an overlay on top of the plan, sketching in the arrangement you have in mind. Freehand sketching is quite satisfactory while you are trying out ideas. When you arrive at a good scheme, carefully draw the symbols using a ruler to measure for the final plan.

It is a good idea not to settle for the first plan or scheme that comes to mind. Although you might come back to the first one, trying a variety of arrangements will help you to arrive at the best solution or to combine a few good features from each of your tryouts.

Any special feature—for instance, a built-in work surface or bookshelves—should be drawn to scale with care while you work on the basic furniture plan.

The final plan should be clearly drawn, even if you have decided to work with templates. Draw the outlines of each template onto the plan. That final plan will serve as a work sheet and, equally important, as a shopping list. Make a couple of copies so you won't lose it; at least one of the copies should have all the crucial dimensions. Carry it with you when you shop for furnishings. You may still be tempted to purchase on impulse, but at least you can check to see if the object will fit the space available.

This brief introduction to planning is followed by a number of sections on types of rooms, each one with both specific suggestions and general recommendations. These room types are organized into more or less conventional settings, although I realize (and indeed I often recommend) that many functions can be combined in the same space. This is particularly true in small homes and in houses or apartments planned on budgets. The first section dealing with living spaces contains more suggestions than any of the succeeding ones. This is because just about everybody needs something called a living space, but not everybody needs, for example, a dining room or a workroom. There are also some comments, where I thought them particularly important, relating to color, lighting, or other elements which are discussed in greater detail later on. I have tried to organize these comments by specific functions but I hope it will be clear that the ideas suggested for any one space are adaptable to any other space or combination of spaces.

Note: The plans throughout Part Two have been reduced to 1/8" = 1'.

PART TWO

ROOM TYPES AND CHECKLISTS

This section presents twelve brief discussions of various room types. Each is followed by a *checklist* of things to consider. The checklist is another tool to facilitate planning and design. The lists are identical in format for each space and are broken down into several categories. They are meant to be examples and obviously cannot apply to every possible situation. I have listed some typical considerations for each space, but I have also left blank spaces at the end so that you can fill in your particular needs and concerns.

The planning aids and checklists are guidelines only. Many people, professionals and consumers alike, prefer to approach design in a less structured way; others meticulously assemble comparative costs from various sources, prepare budget lists, make careful spatial plans, and collect photographs and samples. Whether you choose to use the tools or not is a personal decision. It is my hope that the various suggested planning aids will above all emphasize the advantages of conscious planning for good design.

4/Living Spaces

Whether you live in a house, an apartment, or a loft, you will undoubtedly designate one area as a living room. Of course, much depends upon your needs and life-style, but probably you will want a space where you can talk with friends, read, listen to music, watch television, or just relax. Faced with decisions about what to buy or make and how to arrange things, you would be wise to plan your space with care. In fact, it would be desirable to make a very simple scale drawing of the space like the one on page 29. Caution: think twice before acquiring furnishings on impulse. The result can be lots of furniture that will do nothing for you or for the room.

Most living spaces have a conversation group as the basic focus. However, many rooms are oriented toward a window, a fireplace, a television set, stereo speakers, an attractive piece of furniture, or a work of art. You should keep this in mind when thinking about an arrangement. If there is an attractive view from your window, consider planning your seating group to take advantage of it (and remember that you need not necessarily cover this view with expensive curtains).

Above all, bear in mind that any part of your home should be used comfortably. Having a "front parlor" only for show is an old-fashioned concept. Yet many people still seem to feel that some unwritten rule obliges them to purchase "sets" of furniture or other expensive "time-honored"

/37

A living space, including storage unit and desk. The simple sofa and inexpensive chairs have been planned around a small area rug and unified with a wall-hung shelf.

styles. It is much more interesting to put your own environment together than simply to transpose a group assembled by a manufacturer or furniture store. A "set" of matched furniture or any other conventional fashion (such as a pair of matched end tables or lamps, an elaborate breakfront, lined curtains, valances, wall-to-wall carpeting) is not necessarily good interior design nor is it usually sensible in budgetary terms.

The sample planning arrangements will explain better than words some possible seating groups, but a few specific suggestions should be helpful. The assumption here is that most people are interested in at least some of the

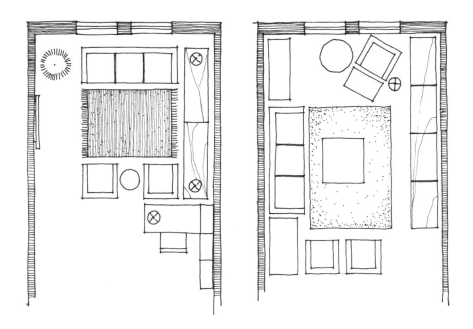

A variety of possible arrangements within the same space.

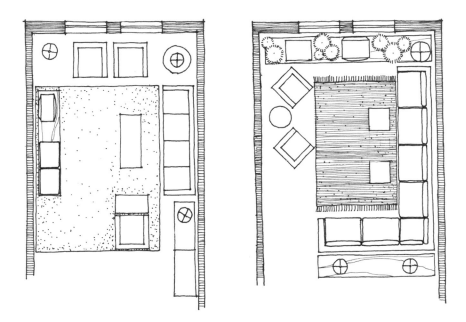

activities in the checklist and that most people do like to have friends visit their homes. Further, I assume that the spaces under discussion are limited in size, since as a rule people with huge houses or apartments do not concern themselves too much with budgets.

A good number of seats for a living space or conversation group is six to eight. Even if the room is large enough to accommodate many more seats in one grouping, it is still difficult to carry on a conversation in a group of more than eight people. As long as the space is adequate, it will be a good idea to plan the seating in such a way that one does not have to scrounge around for folding chairs or ask friends to sit on the floor if a few people drop in. The distance of about 10 feet from chair to chair or chair to sofa is comfortable for conversation. It is also about the right distance for watching television or listening to music.

In planning a conversation group, it is important to arrange the seating in such a way that people can see each other or see a focal point (view, television, fireplace) but to leave space for leg room and passage. Placing two seating units (sofa and chair, or two chairs) corner to corner at right angles leaves no room to stretch legs. Wherever possible some "breathing" space, such as that shown in the drawings, will make a more pleasant grouping. Coffee tables or end tables are usually needed for drinks, food, or ashtrays. To reach a coffee table from a sofa, try to allow approximately 12 inches of space between the front edge of the sofa or chair and the table. If your sofa is rather long, with a long coffee table in front, the person sitting in the center may find it difficult to get in and out of his seat. In such cases, two or three smaller tables in front of the sofa may be a better solution.

In order to demonstrate the least expensive solutions to seating problems, the sample plans show arrangements with relatively small area rugs. (Wall-to-wall carpeting and large rugs obviously represent a greater investment.) If you plan to use area rugs, keep in mind that furniture should be either on the rug or off. Anything standing half on and half off will be wobbly and will look strange. Often a small rug can successfully pull a seating group together as a unit, especially in interiors where other functions must be accommodated or other areas created within the same space.

The checklist you will prepare for the living space should make clear what other special functions are to be incorporated in the room. It is not only appropriate but frequently more interesting to give your living room a very personal quality. If it must double as a study, library, or workroom, you need not camouflage these functions. A stamp of personal expression can be achieved by simply following your needs. A room can be quite beautiful if furnished with an absolute minimum of furniture, or with the addition of a desk, bookshelves, or eating space. The dullest rooms are those that look like settings in a furniture store or model apartment, waiting for people to move in and give some character to the place.

The actual furniture may sometimes be the least important component of a well-designed room. Many young people prefer to sit on the floor. Spaces consciously planned for that can be very handsome, with color, wall hangings, plants, prints, or other special decorative devices enhancing them and even making them elegant. There are also ways to create uniquely designed environments without any traditional furnishings at all. But such seating platforms, levels, and specially built areas within a conventional space require a good deal of design ability. People who wish to attempt such a setting should seek some professional guidance from a designer.

I have been assuming that your living space is fairly small. But the same arrangements apply for large spaces; you could have two or even three groupings, or combine the living space with one or more other functions, such as study or dining. If there is room for two seating groups, it is a good idea to make one larger and more dominant, with the smaller one designed for two to four people. A fireplace or a bay window, for instance, might accommodate just two comfortable chairs for private conversation, while the larger grouping would be more suitable for those occasions when there are several people in the room.

A very important consideration in all planning is the circulation or traffic pattern. Wherever possible, furniture should be placed so that one does not have to walk in front of chairs, or through the center of a seating group. If the space is very small, you may want to reduce furnishings to a minimum in order to avoid constant cross-traffic. This is particularly important if more than two people live in the home and if there are children. A plan that forces you to walk through the middle of the living room when you enter with a bag of groceries or when you take out the kitchen garbage creates inconvenience as well as maintenance problems (footprints, spilled liquids, etc.).

The actual choice of furnishings is really quite easy once the planning and functional considerations have been thought out. You can create a handsome room with simple contemporary furnishings, or with old pieces found, inherited, or bought at auction. Some of the most attractive combinations can be achieved with a variety of styles. The major seating pieces, such as sofas and large chairs, are usually available in simple, timeless contemporary

A living space designed on two levels, including built-in seating and carpeting wrapped around platforms and bases for seats. Storage units have been designed as integral parts of the environment. This kind of design approach requires professional skills.

designs at fairly reasonable prices. Since sofas tend to be costly, you might even avoid them altogether. A simple foam rubber mattress on a neatly built bench can take the place of a sofa, as can a daybed (box spring and mattress) if not too wide, with an interesting cover or throw. Wedge-shaped foam bolsters can provide adequate back support for such arrangements. The point is that there is no need to spend a lot of money on a bulky, ornate sofa. Really comfortable, well-designed contemporary chairs can also be rather expensive, so you might consider an older overstuffed chair or even an old wing chair in an otherwise modern setting. The comfort factor is not as crucial for the two or three additional chairs used occasionally for guests. A lighter, less padded chair is perfectly fine for an evening of conversation.

A good approach to the selection of furniture might be to spend more money on just one or two really well-designed pieces to start off with. Owning a few good pieces and replacing some of the makeshift ones over the years could give you a very satisfying collection of good modern design when you are through. If you like period furnishings, it is possible to buy some at auctions or in "junk" or thrift shops. A couple of interesting old chairs or tables or other smaller pieces, together with fairly simple, classic contemporary furniture, can make a far more successful combination than a whole set of mediocre reproductions.

The same approach can be followed with carpeting and lamps. Wall-to-wall carpeting is always rather expensive. If your home is not a permanent one, the investment is usually a total loss when you move. Instead, you might choose a very plush and luxuriously textured area rug or perhaps a patterned or woven design such as the Scandinavian rugs, or an old Oriental rug bought at a country auction. Any of these can be a focal point in the room and will have the advantage of being movable.

A good deal of excellent modern lighting is available; some of it is inexpensive (see the section on lighting, p. 170). A living space lit with the simplest architectural floodlamps, or clip-on or reflected lights, can be immeasurably enhanced by one or two attractive modern lamps or more traditional bases with shades. For a living space, the key to lighting should be flexibility, good distribution, no glare, and illumination for reading or work in those areas where it is needed. Good lighting distribution simply requires several sources of light, placed strategically around the room. One very bright lamp may provide enough general illumination, but it will also be glaring and uncomfortable on the eyes. The luxury of one or two extra pools of light is often a pleasant visual touch, even if such accents do not contribute much to the total illumination in the room.

Although color is discussed in a later chapter, it is such an integral part of the design of the room that something must be said about it here. A white or close-to-white color for the walls and ceilings is always a good choice. However, the best rule about color might be that there are no rules. Some people have an instinctive sense of color and like strong tones, and indeed there are some excellent rooms painted in intense dark colors. An intense or lively background color can be fine—but it can also be difficult to handle and to live with. Perhaps the least successful rooms are those painted in dull, pastel "builder's" colors. A really strong and vibrant color in one area, on one wall, in the floor covering, or in the curtains, can give more sparkle to a room for less money than if the entire room is painted in the identical shade. Dark colors absorb light, so the least expensive way to brighten a room is with white walls and white ceilings. As for the choice of colors for fabric, curtains, and rugs, the best guideline is to use just one or two colors instead of a rainbow. If you are really puzzled about color choices, earth colors and warm neutral colors, such as beiges and browns and whites, are always a good general background, with accents perhaps in pumpkin, orange, blue, yellow, or green. Some excellent decorators have made their reputations on daring and often clashing color schemes, but unless you are lucky enough to have an instinctive color sense, the fewer colors the better.

Having stated that the actual selection of furniture can be the least important part of a good interior, I must add that some visual delight or something of interest should happen in a good room. Rooms with architectural interest (a view, a fireplace, bay windows) are easy to deal with. But the normal, boxlike room needs more than just a few pieces of minimal furniture. Probably few people who are interested in budget design have extensive art collections, and it is not necessary to have them for visual interest. Prints and graphics are popular, and there are many relatively inexpensive sources for graphics. (More about graphics, art, and accessories on pp. 191-200.) You can also introduce some excitement by hanging or stretching a piece of fabric as a major decorative element. Reasonably priced printed fabrics, such as India prints, Mexican cotton, or simple rugs made into wall hangings, might be considered. Plants provide some of the least expensive and most interesting decorative touches. Personal and sometimes unorthodox accessories such as baskets, supergraphics, found objects, or memorabilia can be enjoyable, inexpensive touches.

All too often, maintenance factors and simple wear and tear are neglected in planning living areas. In selecting materials and furnishings remember that a comfortable chair that will be used frequently should not be covered in a delicate, light-colored fabric. Perhaps an extra chair might be covered in something impractical, but as a rule upholstery and table surfaces, curtains and floor coverings, are meant to be lived with and should not have to be treated like museum pieces. The custom of covering fabrics with plastic covers is happily on the wane—they look cold and uninviting and are extremely uncomfortable. In fact, the concept of slipcovers in general seems somewhat overrated. Since upholstered furniture will wear out in time as a result of sagging or broken springs, broken frames, or dried-up foam rubber, the life expectancy of a piece of furniture does not really double with a set of slipcovers. If you have an attractive room, it seems much more sensible to use it and worry about recovering and replacing things in due time. However, if a fabric should wear out before the whole piece needs reupholstering, slipcovers often represent a real cost saving. The labor for slipcovers is far less than for stripping down a sofa or chair and reupholstering it completely. The further advantage of slipcovers is that they can be removed for cleaning—a particular plus for families with young children.

A final word of advice: there are no set regulations; anyone who has special needs or who wishes to incorporate some special features should never feel constrained by nonexistent rules. If you like to paint, there is no reason why a studio area cannot be incorporated right into the living room. If you want a small planting or greenhouse area, why not include that? And if your apartment is a small efficiency unit, there is no reason why a bed must be hidden or pushed out of the way. Covered with a throw, it can provide lots of seating for friends. A living space with the emphasis on living will usually be better designed than one created for show.

CHECKLIST Some Recommended Considerations for LIVING SPACES

PRIMARY FUNCTIONS—ACTIVITIES
How many people should normally be seated comfortably?_____
How many people can space hold without becoming crowded? _____
What activities do you plan for the space? _____
    Listening to music? _____
    Watching television? _____
    Reading? _____
    Viewing slides or movies? _____

SECONDARY FUNCTIONS
Space for guests to sleep? _____
Parties or playing cards? _____
Space for eating? _____
Making music? _____
Studying? _____
Working on projects? _____

SPECIAL CONSIDERATIONS
Storing books or records?_____
Space for a piano or storage for bulky objects? _____
Space for special interests such as plants, print
    display, or dancing? _____

NOTES ON COLOR, MATERIALS, LIGHTING, ETC.
Reading lights? _____
Accent lights? _____
Area rug?_____
Artwork?_____

OTHER_____
_____
_____
_____

5/Eating Spaces

Formal dining rooms are rarely found in small apartments, but most apartments and houses have some space which is naturally planned or suited for eating. Where there is a separate room, a dining "L," or a space such as a dining foyer, the requirements are similar. It is important to realize that a delightful and useful dining area can be created without buying a complete set of matched furniture. Often some of the standard pieces that come in such a set are not really needed even if you do have a separate dining room.

Just about every home will need a table. Its shape and size should follow the dimensions and proportions of the room. Although the actual shape of the table represents a personal preference, a round surface tends to be somewhat more social. In many areas, however, the only logical choice is a rectangular or oval table.

The height of all dining tables is pretty much standard—approximately 29 inches—but the other dimensions are almost unlimited. The exact space requirement depends on how elaborate a setting is desired, or how closely you are willing to squeeze together while eating. The rule of thumb is to allow a space approximately 2 feet wide per person (1 foot 10 inches is minimum, but somewhat crowded). Round tables range from 30 inches in diameter, for two persons, to 54 inches, for six (comfortably) or up to eight (somewhat squeezed).

/47

Rectangular tables usually have a minimum width of 30 inches, and the length varies from 48 to 72 inches. Ideally, a rectangular table should be at least 30 x 60 inches to seat six people comfortably. To enable two people to sit together at the head (narrow end) of the table, the minimum width should be close to 48 inches. These dimensions can also be used in figuring the maximum seating for square, boat-shaped, or oval tables, with the qualification that oval tables do not accommodate more than one person at the head.

For small spaces, and particularly for those dining areas that are used infrequently for larger groups, extension tables can be a real advantage. In very small apartments, storing extension leaves can be a problem; you might consider a table with a self-storing leaf. There are also some handsome and reasonably priced dropleaf tables; the "Scandinavian-style" dropleaf tables (below) are especially practical and inexpensive. A few manufacturers make convertible tables which can be lowered to coffee-table height and raised to dining height. That solution is recommended only for the very small space without alternatives, since the mechanism of these tables might not always operate easily and the surface usually has to be cleared before changing the height.

A well-designed, inexpensive dropleaf table.

Dining chairs come in all shapes, styles, and sizes. Make sure that the chairs are dining (or desk) height and that they can be pushed under the table if your space is limited. This might mean that armchairs cannot be used. As it is, side chairs are less expensive and are perfectly comfortable for eating. However, if you do have adequate space, the advantage of an armchair is that it can be a comfortable extra seat to use elsewhere and for those who like to linger around a table after meals.

Both tables and chairs should be selected with an eye to maintenance. A plastic laminated top is especially easy to maintain. If the warmth and richness of wood is desired, an oil finish needs only an occasional oiling or waxing; it can even be sanded down if it gets badly marked. Glass or marble tables cost more and are harder to maintain, and special materials such as slate are usually very expensive. Sturdy butcher-block tops are a reasonably priced solution, but they are heavy to move and are not available as extension tables.

The upholstery material for dining chairs must be carefully selected for practicality—especially if there are children. A good sturdy woven fabric can take a fair amount of abuse; a silk, satin, or light-colored damask cannot. Plastic fabrics, such as naugahyde, stand up well; leather is very expensive. You might also consider chairs with cane or rush seats and wooden or plastic chairs. These chairs are among the most reasonable, and some of them come in very handsome designs. (See p. 127 for more on chairs.)

Mixing furniture styles can be interesting to look at and can save a great deal of money. Consider a plastic laminate (such as Formica) table on a simple base, surrounded by more elegant (perhaps carved) chairs, or an old Victorian round oak table (from a thrift shop) surrounded by very contemporary chairs, or perhaps the combination of a glass-top table on a simple steel frame base, with cane bentwood chairs. A sideboard need not be specifically made for a dining room. A chest of drawers (perhaps an old one) or a cabinet with sliding doors can do the same job and might be more interesting. One of the least expensive tables is a set of sawhorses with a flush door on top. Or you might attach four steel legs bought in a hardware store to a piece of wood. It is even possible to mix the chairs. You might begin by buying four side chairs and add two armchairs at a later date. As long as the armchairs are compatible with the other chairs in spirit and scale, the mixture might turn out to be particularly interesting.

One or two major points must be considered when planning a dining area. If possible, the table should be close to the kitchen. If your living room is large enough, you can define the eating space with a freestanding cabinet or the back of a sofa or chairs. Many of the room dividers on the market are expensive and bulky; however, if a room is large enough and a divider can be used for storage, it is certainly worth considering. But if the kitchen is large and the dining area is rarely used, then it might be better to have the living or work areas closer to the cooking area. If you prefer to eat most of your meals in the kitchen, by all means do so, and use the conventional eating area for a work space or play area—whatever you need (see p. 52).

Try to arrange the table for comfortable access to the chairs and for easy serving. If your dining area is very small, you may have to settle for squeezing on those occasions when you entertain six or eight dinner guests.

Keep in mind that a dining table does not have to be centered in an area, especially in an informal setting. A rectangular table, for instance, looks and works well when "teed" off a wall. It will provide space for four or five people and take up considerably less space than if it were freestanding (see p. 90).

The checklist on page 55 will help you decide what other kinds of furnishings you might need for your dining area. In a formal dining room there may be enough room for a hutch, a credenza, or a breakfront; but be wary—most of these pieces are expensive. Unless you have many dishes, glasses, or wedding gifts to store, a relatively small cabinet might be the best solution. A chest of drawers or cabinet with doors or a door/drawer combination can easily be found at a height of 30 to 34 inches—a good height for serving. There are also some inexpensive wall-hung cabinets on the market, which look light and graceful, particularly in small spaces. If you do not need a large amount of storage space, a serving cart or wall-mounted shelf (console) may be adequate; if the space is very limited, no additional furnishings at all might be best.

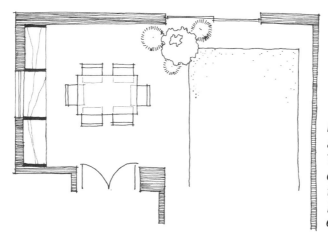

Plan of the apartment dining area shown on page 51. The built-in storage unit creates a framing effect for the window, as well as providing space for radiator enclosure under window.

Dining area, illustrated in plan on page 50. The commercial stacking chairs are extremely handsome and effective and reasonably priced. The window is covered with vertical blinds, and track lighting illuminates all areas of the room.

If you do have a lot of space or use the kitchen for most meals, consider using the dining area for some additional purpose, such as a place for a desk, or a reading retreat with a large, comfortable armchair, a lamp, and small table, or a decorative planting area. If the dining table will have to double as a place for writing or studying, consider adding bookshelves to the eating area. When most meals are eaten in the kitchen or breakfast area, a formal dining room may be used only a few hours each month. If you figure out the rental cost per square foot for such wasted space, you will see why putting that area to another use makes sense!

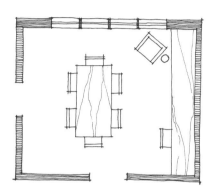

Plan of a dining room suggesting the possibility of a counter or storage system to double as a study area.

In addition to functional considerations, aesthetic ones must also be weighed for a dining area. The most dramatic effect can be achieved with color. In an L-shaped dining space, for instance, you might paint the end wall a strong accent color, or cover one wall with fabric, grasscloth, cork, or wallpaper. If you own some graphics, paintings, photographs, or wall hangings, a carefully placed arrangement of these might be a possibility. Or one good-sized wall hanging (perhaps something very inexpensive such as a Mexican blanket) might add warmth. Indoor plants massed in a group near a window, perhaps combined with hanging plants or plants on window sills, can be most attractive.

Or consider simply installing a wall-hung shelf right across one wall. It could double as a serving surface and a display place for plants or pottery.

It is always nice to have a few personal objects on display. This need not be the traditional expensive china. Use simple ceramic pieces (you can get

Dining room with bay window using plants and salvaged stained glass in place of curtains. An old pedestal table has been combined with classic contemporary chairs. The wall holding the floating counter has been painted a contrasting color.

original ceramics for very little money in small craft shops and at crafts fairs) or old bottles or candlesticks from antique or "junk" shops. That kind of personal decoration is usually more effective than a ready-made "centerpiece."

Many people feel that a formal chandelier is essential for a proper dining room. While there are very interesting lighting fixtures, both old and new, specifically created for dining, they tend to be costly. If you are stuck with an ugly ceiling light provided by the building owner, perhaps the cheapest way of dealing with it is to replace it with an inexpensive flush-mounted globe light or a "lighting can" (a surface-mounted cylindrical spot in painted metal finish). Both fixtures will be more effective on a dimmer control switch. A simple globe shape is far better than a copy of a period chandelier. Often there is no ceiling light at all. It is possible to create a very handsome effect with a large parchment Japanese lantern. Since these globes or "bubbles" are very lightweight, they can be installed easily on a simple ceiling hook. In private houses, it is often possible to recess a spotlight ("Hi Hat") into the ceiling. A dimmer is worth considering for almost any dining room fixture; it costs just a few dollars and can normally be substituted for an ordinary light switch. Use real candles for festive atmosphere. (See p. 170 for more on lighting.)

A final word on eating spaces: be careful that you don't overdo on the furniture by trying to crowd too much of it into too little space.

CHECKLIST Some Recommended Considerations for EATING SPACES

PRIMARY FUNCTIONS—ACTIVITIES
Formal dining (if you have space for it)?_____

Informal dining? _____

How many people can be seated—4, 6, 8, 10, 12? _____

How often will you need maximum seating? _____

All your meals in dining space, or only on some occasions? _____

SECONDARY FUNCTIONS
Study or work? _____

Reading and sitting? _____

Object display? _____

Space for indoor plants? _____

SPECIAL CONSIDERATIONS
Lots of storage for dishes? _____

A surface for serving buffet-style dinners? _____

NOTES ON COLOR, MATERIALS, LIGHTING, ETC.
Center fixture or dimmers? _____

Wall covering or paint for part of room or all walls?_____

Leave floor as is or refinish it? _____

OTHER _____

_____

_____

_____

_____

_____

_____

_____

_____

_____

_____

6/Entry/Foyer

Most entry areas are small and need to serve several functions. A place to hang coats is the number-one requirement. If there is no closet, coat hooks or a clothes tree will do. You can get some inexpensive but attractive coat hooks in a hardware store and mount them on a nice piece of wood, or you can find any number of coat hooks already mounted on a surface and ready for installation. If you have room for a clothes tree, consider looking for something like a bentwood tree or an old one with character.

A mirror is a good idea too. Most people like to check their appearance before going out or when entering your home. A small mirror should suffice, but it should be decorative—perhaps an old one, or a well-designed contemporary one.

If the space is large enough, there will be room for some kind of chest or cabinet which could double as a handy surface for putting packages down and extra storage for scarves, gloves, boots, and so on. Some other possible furnishings are indicated in the checklist. If there is no space for any kind of furniture, consider a wall-hung shelf, or a "floating" shelf such as the one in the illustration on page 58.

If you do not have a separate entry area, you can create the feeling of one. For example, the backs of two chairs or of a sofa can form a divider between the door and the main living space. Perhaps you could hang some fabric, macrame, a print, or a painting from the ceiling in order to screen the living space from the entrance.

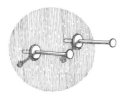

Attractive coat hooks are available for use in a foyer.

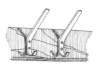

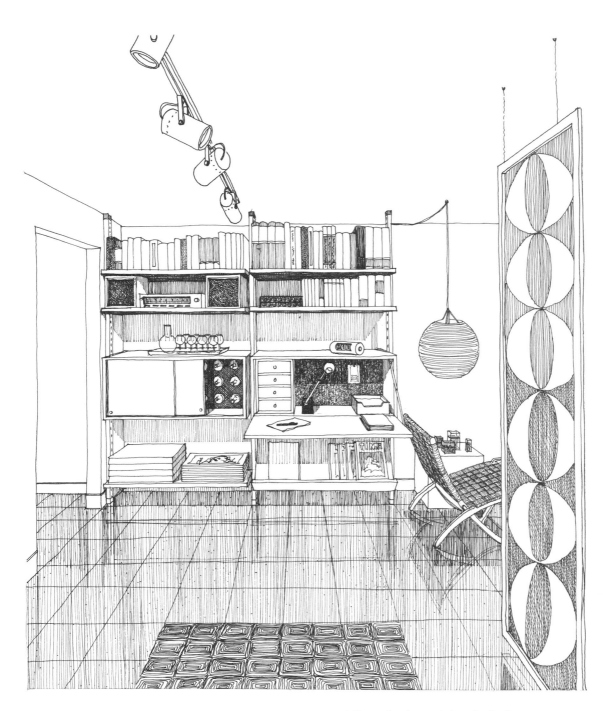

An apartment foyer containing a storage wall holding desk and bookshelves. Separation from main living space has been created with a hanging fabric print and the placement of a chair.

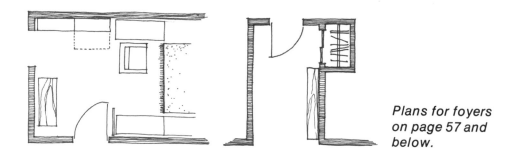

Plans for foyers on page 57 and below.

You can set the style and mood of your home with paintings, graphics, photographs, or furniture if there is room. If your entry is a hallway, it might become a small display gallery.

Consider appropriate lighting, especially if you choose to make your entry a gallery. Most builders provide an absolute minimum. Adequate wattage is needed to view objects in a gallery, and it might be desirable to buy a new fixture with increased wattage or, even better, track lighting, the type of fixture normally used for gallery lighting.

A strong color (perhaps even an intense color on the ceiling), supergraphics, or some lively wall covering can give a dramatic and delightful character to the space.

A narrow foyer showing one wall covered with large graphics or mural. A narrow floating shelf is the only "furniture" used. Three simple parchment globes have been used for lighting.

CHECKLIST Some Recommended Considerations for ENTRY/FOYER

PRIMARY FUNCTIONS—ACTIVITIES
Closet?_____

Guest closet? _____

If no closet, then coat rack or hooks? _____

Mirror? _____

Shelf or surface to put down handbags, mail, or packages? _____

SECONDARY FUNCTIONS
Space for some special function or furniture?_____

Room for some seating for putting on galoshes and boots? _____

SPECIAL CONSIDERATIONS
Room for extra storage? _____

   Baby carriage? _____

   Bicycles? _____

   Shopping cart, etc.? _____

NOTES ON COLOR, MATERIALS, LIGHTING, ETC.
Special color on walls or ceiling? _____

Doormat or small rug? _____

Lighting for artwork? _____

OTHER _____

_____

_____

_____

_____

_____

_____

_____

_____

_____

_____

7/Den/Study/ Family Room

A formal study is a rarity in small houses or apartments. The family room or den is usually found in contemporary suburban homes, not in houses where the prime emphasis is on low cost.

Certainly, a separate room for special activities is a great luxury. However, I believe it is usually more functional and economical to combine "family room" activities with those that take place in other areas. Try to use all the spaces in your home to best advantage. A showplace living room tends to force too many other functions into the family room or study, with less than satisfactory results for both rooms.

A family room is for informal living. Basically, the design, the furnishings, and the materials should all be selected with that in mind. A resilient tile or wood floor with an area rug makes for easy maintenance. Any table should be equally suitable for card games, childrens' homework, informal eating, or crafts projects (a wood finish or a plastic laminate table top can take just about any abuse). Since the room will probably be used for a variety of functions, choose lightweight furniture that can be pushed around or even cleared out of the room for a party. If you plan to watch television or listen to music, arrange the seating at the proper viewing or listening distance.

Often, the best results are achieved with some kind of building in or "custom design." Books, records, a music system, a television, a liquor cabinet, a desk, and a variety of storage needs can all be accommodated in a wall storage system. The example shown here is further explained under "Built-in Furniture" (p. 143). It is just one of many possible ways of creating your own storage wall or having a local cabinetmaker build it. Many stores sell component parts of wall "systems" which the layman can easily arrange and install. Make sure to check the dimensions for books, records, stereo equipment, and other components before building a storage wall; you will find some of the standard measurements listed under "Built-in Furniture," and you will want to measure your own before going ahead with a building project.

The plan here is for a small combination study/family room. Obviously your room will not have the identical shape, but certain features, such as one unbroken wall as the best location for a storage wall, are easily adapted to almost any space. A game table should measure at least 32 x 32 inches to be suitable for card games, and unless you wish to use a very inexpensive folding table (perhaps covered with a large tablecloth), a Parsons table is a good choice. Chairs could be inexpensive ones, perhaps painted bentwood as suggested in the sketch. In the example shown, there would be no need for an additional desk chair. If you do not want to buy a sofa or sofa-bed, use a simple box spring and mattress—with a throw, wedge-shaped bolsters, and throw pillows—for a comfortable sofa. Some foam rubber sofas have back bolsters which can be taken off to convert the sofa into a bed. Or you might consider one of the sofas shown under "Classic Makeshifts" (p. 159)—a do-it-yourself project involving a flush door and a foam mattress. To really pare the budget, use two "director's" chairs as armchairs. The fact that these chairs sell for under $20 apiece does not make them any less attractive. The small stack tables pictured could be used both as corner tables and as coffee tables. An area rug, some artwork, wall hangings, or other decorative touches would complete such a room for a minimum budget.

Parsons table

Plan of family room shown on page 62.

A small family room with storage wall. Table has a pedestal base used for restaurant tables, with a round white plastic laminate top. Bentwood chairs around table and two canvas director's chairs are well designed and inexpensive possibilities. The three small stack tables can double as coffee tables.

CHECKLIST Some Recommended Considerations for
DEN/STUDY/FAMILY ROOM

PRIMARY FUNCTIONS—ACTIVITIES
Is space completely separate from other living space? _____
Emphasis on desk work (study, etc)? _____
Need for table—eating or playing cards?_____
Should room be retreat for reading or listening? _____

SECONDARY FUNCTIONS
Guest room? _____
Hobbies (sewing, weaving, TV, etc.)? _____
Play area for children? _____

SPECIAL CONSIDERATIONS
Shelving for books, TV, stereo, records, tapes?_____
Large parties or cocktail parties? _____
Liquor storage? _____

NOTES ON COLOR, MATERIALS, LIGHTING, ETC.
Area rug?_____
Wall covering, cork? _____
Special reading lights? _____

OTHER _____
_____
_____
_____
_____
_____
_____
_____
_____
_____
_____
_____

8/Sleeping Spaces/ Bedrooms

Let's vary the old formula of a formal bedroom with a large bed centered in the room, two matching night tables, two dressers, with perhaps a tall chest, and a mirror hung over the dressers. There are other solutions that are more practical, attractive and economical.

An example of unconventional bedroom design is something like a sleeping loft. This idea is rather ingenious in small spaces, but it does require a higher-than-average ceiling. It also requires a fair amount of skill in construction, and it assumes that the sleeping area is just that—an area, rather than a separate room.

Plan of two levels of loft bedroom shown on page 65.

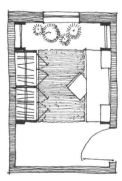 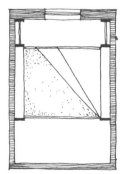

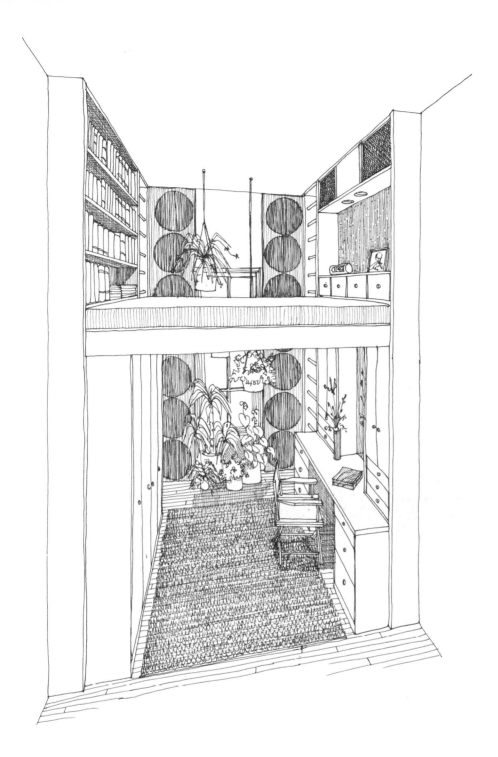

A loft bedroom can be considered only in buildings with high ceilings. Closet, storage system, and desk are built in. Loft bed is reached by ladder incorporated into storage wall.

A traditional bedroom plan, arranged well for traffic and floor space.

In a more conventional bedroom, place the bed or beds toward one side or toward a corner to increase the available floor space. When planning the arrangement, take into account the access to closets and to the bathroom, as well as to the bed itself. Another basic decision is whether to emphasize decoration or function. If you plan to use the room for work, study, reading, sewing, or watching television, these considerations will give the space its special character. If you have no need to use the room for additional activities, then some simple decorative ideas can enhance it.

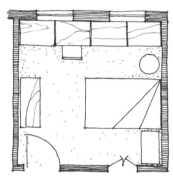

Plan of bedroom shown on page 67.

The least expensive way to create interest is with paint. Usually there is at least one unbroken wall in a room, which would be the most suitable place for the beds in conventional arrangements. A fairly dramatic effect can be achieved by painting that wall a strong color and keeping the other walls white or light. A strong accent color on one surface is most effective as a background for beds. Instead of the bed dominating the room with its bulk,

A bedroom-study combination. Rattan headboard, rattan chest/night table, and matchstick bamboo shades are all inexpensive features.

the color effect takes over. It is important that such an accent wall does not have windows, doors, or other architectural elements breaking the painted surface plane. If you use a wall covering for that one wall—perhaps a textured or a vinyl paper—you might also eliminate the need for a headboard. If you do want to use a headboard, you can make a very simple one by using plywood or Masonite covered tightly with a stretched fabric. This can be attached to the wall with just two nails or screws.

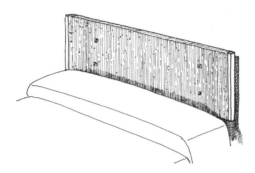

A simple but effective headboard can be made by wrapping fabric around a piece of plywood as shown. Headboard can be wall-hung.

Even with a conventional plan, two different night tables might be more interesting and cheaper than matching ones. A simple round table on one side of the bed can hold telephone, radio, clock, and would give you extra storage. The inexpensive Oriental basket chests make good bedside surfaces and provide storage for extra blankets at the same time.

Chests of drawers vary enormously in price, but those that are part of a regular bedroom set are usually fairly high. On the other hand, old furniture and refinished furniture is always relatively inexpensive. There are also a number of stores featuring unfinished furniture; chests of drawers in particular are good buys and can be covered with a clear shellac or painted. Add to that an inexpensive low round table, a rattan chest, a homemade headboard, and a chair, maybe an old rocker, and your total furniture budget could be considerably less than the cost of a single fancy dresser.

Floor covering can be a major expense. For ease of maintenance as well as comfort, many people insist on wall-to-wall carpeting in their bedrooms. If you do want that luxury, use inexpensive cotton or acrylic carpeting, since the traffic in bedrooms usually does not require the strength of material that you need in other areas. However, if you have a nice floor, you can just use small rugs in front of the bed.

A colorful bedspread can do much to enhance a bedroom. Since it is one of the major areas of color, you might consider an Indian cotton throw. They come in interesting patterns and good colors and cost very little. Department stores sell a good variety of bedspreads; often the reasonably priced ones are better designed than the elaborately tailored and ruffled ones. Bedroom windows need shades or blinds for privacy and light control. Frequently the shape and placement of windows is irregular and presents a difficult problem. If you want a soft, luxurious effect, a wall-to-wall and floor-to-ceiling curtain might camouflage the poor placement of windows. The least expensive treatment consists of readymade curtains; with luck they will fit. There are a number of prepleated tapes and similar devices which can be used to make your own curtains. A simple fabric, such as a plain cotton, can be a very effective choice. Today's patterned bed sheets make attractive curtains with a minimum of sewing and expense. Other inexpensive window treatments are discussed on page 178. If there are windows on two walls, a treatment carried over adjoining walls can be very effective and at the same time provide a natural setting for the bed. Anything like this requires a good deal of fabric, however, and unless you can find inexpensive yardage or readymade curtains, the suggestion might be too expensive. In that case the simplest curtains, or no curtains at all, would be better.

Hanging lights such as the ones shown in the sketch are attractive but may be difficult to install. Desk or drafting lamps are handy, especially since they can be controlled so that one person may read in bed without disturbing the other one. Pin-up lights are equally useful and inexpensive.

The extra functions of a bedroom depend entirely upon your needs. A combination bedroom-study makes sense. Built-in storage/desk spaces and bookshelves can be created with simple chests, flush doors, and wall-hung shelves, or a similar system can be assembled from the readymade parts and pieces carried in stores specializing in furniture components.

A word about beds—presumably the key element of most bedrooms: a good mattress is one of the few home furnishings where a bargain may turn out to be an expensive mistake. Here you get what you pay for. The only way expense can be cut is to eliminate the box spring, especially if you prefer sleeping on a hard surface. Many people buy a box spring and mattress as a matter of tradition and then spend more money on a bedboard to obtain a harder surface. A mattress placed directly on the floor will give you firm support; at the same time, the low scale will make the room look less crowded. There are some well-designed platform beds available, and if you are ambitious you can make your own platform fairly easily (see p. 141).

The last sketch shows how an extra corner or pocket in a closet can be fitted for shelves and perhaps supplemented with a cheap cardboard chest from the notions section of a department store.

A simple way of increasing usable closet space.

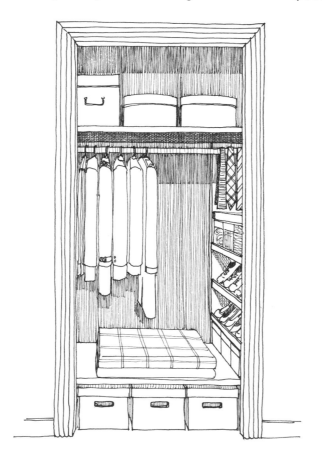

CHECKLIST Some Recommended Considerations for
SLEEPING SPACES / BEDROOMS

PRIMARY FUNCTIONS—ACTIVITIES

Type of bed: double, twin, Harvard frame, platform,
    waterbed? _____

Size of bed or beds? _____

Size of headboard, if any? _____

Is there enough closet space? _____

Can closet be added? _____

Can closet be fitted with shelves? _____

SECONDARY FUNCTIONS

Chests of drawers or cabinets for storage? _____

Surface near beds? _____

Study, work, sewing, etc.? _____

SPECIAL CONSIDERATIONS

Full-length mirror? Perhaps another one? _____

A place to sit, to store your bedspread at night, to
    hang clothing? _____

A dressing table? _____

NOTES ON COLOR, MATERIALS, LIGHTING, ETC.

Light for reading in bed? _____

Other kinds of lighting? _____

Light-proof shades? _____

OTHER _____

_____
_____
_____
_____
_____
_____
_____

9/ Children's Rooms

The obvious truth that children grow up rapidly is often forgotten when furnishing a baby's room, especially for the first child. The results often force teen-age children to live in "cute" babylike rooms without the facilities they really need. Especially for the budget-conscious family, a clear plan will help curb the impulse to buy furnishings that will be outgrown in no time at all.

Buy as little as possible for a baby's room. Typical baby furniture outgrows its usefulness as quickly as the infant becomes a toddler. Very simple and inexpensive pieces (a crib, a bassinet, a chest), perhaps "handed down" from relatives or friends and painted in cheerful colors, should be all the furniture you need. A bright color or a lively wall covering (on the ceiling too, perhaps) can give you a cheerful and pleasant room. The real furnishing needs for a child's room start when he begins to be more independent, and at that point you might as well plan the room for the future. The best examples of design for children's rooms are European. There is indeed a difference in scale and design which makes certain furniture more appropriate to children; but it should not be "cutesy." The best children's furniture can literally grow with the child: chairs and tables that adjust to different heights, and storage units which can be added to as the child grows.

An example of the bad features that mar so much of our traditional children's furniture are the toy chests with lids that can hurt a child and which

Some examples of well-designed children's furniture. The trundle bed can of course be used in guest rooms as well.

are built in such a way that he or she cannot possibly look in and find what he wants buried at the bottom. A better alternative is simple, open, cube-type storage units. They are very inexpensive and make it possible for a child to find what he is looking for; the same units can later be used to store games or records. Of course, there are also many sturdy, well-designed modular storage units and units that form desks and work surfaces. If you start with one or two of these, you can add more over the years as the child's needs shift. Wall-hung shelves, too, are generally suitable for children's rooms.

The best of all of these units have a "forgiving" quality. Hardwood, plastic laminates, and plastic furniture can be crayoned, spilled upon, and generally mistreated without permanent damage.

Since most children's rooms are limited in size, a carefully considered plan is important. Whether the room is for one child or two, it probably makes sense to allow for an extra bed. Bunk beds are a favorite and they conserve floor space. Trundle beds are a good choice for accommodating sleepover company. If two children use the room, consider placing twin beds at right angles to each other. That way, with the use of some wedge-shaped bolsters, the beds can be used for sitting during the daytime, and the space in the center of the room can be used for a play area.

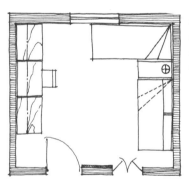

A plan for a room for two children. Placing beds at right angles creates a conversation area for a group of children and extra floor space for play.

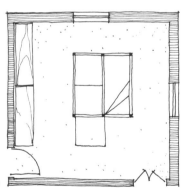

Plan of child's room shown on page 75.

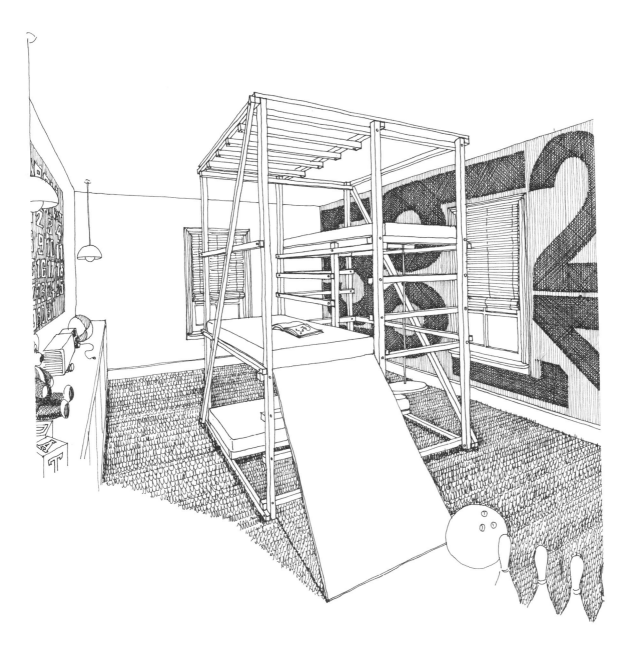

A child's room using a freestanding play/sleep module. More often than not this sort of design requires professional ability, but there are a few units of this type available readymade. Notice the use of supergraphics on one wall.

Many exciting and delightful designs can be created for children, including special environments, places to climb, freestanding upper-level beds with desks and seating below, and so forth. These ideas are expensive to execute, however, even if you build them yourself. I mention them only to point out the possibilities; many examples have been illustrated in magazines and books and in model rooms.

An area of cork or tack board will give the child a place to pin up pictures or posters. Upson board and Homasote, the least expensive tack boards, come in standard 4 x 8-foot sheets. Heavy cork is a somewhat more decorative material. Cork tiles come in cartons and can be glued directly to wall surfaces with a special glue. These cork tiles, usually made of Portuguese cork, are a dark brown color and provide a handsome texture. The exposed edges are brittle and liable to break, so take care to protect the edges or to apply the cork between two walls or projections.

No single flooring material is best for all children. Wall-to-wall carpeting, area rugs, wood floors, or tile floors may be equally good, depending on the age and interests of the child. Since children are apt to sit on the floor a great deal, carpeting represents an advantage. Tightly woven carpeting, or the indoor-outdoor type, can be used as a playing surface and cleaned more easily than higher-pile carpeting. Carpet tiles are often on sale, are easy to install, and can be replaced if an accident should mar one or two tiles.

Good lighting is important for everybody, but especially for children. No matter what kind of lighting the room has, a good desk lamp or drafting lamp is definitely worth the money. The children's desks available commercially are often too small for normal housework or research projects. If you cannot afford a large desk, you might place the smaller desk surface in such a way that it adjoins a chest or cabinet, thus extending the work surface. (See pp. 78-80, 138, and 147-151 for work ideas.)

Lastly, I would stress that children should be encouraged to participate in any decisions affecting their own rooms. Of course you may, in the end, be forced to use your parental prerogative to veto choices that are impractical or expensive!

CHECKLIST Some Recommended Considerations for
CHILDREN'S ROOMS

PRIMARY FUNCTIONS—ACTIVITIES
One child or more than one?_____
Emphasis on play, games, study, or reading?_____
Storage needs: toys, books, dolls, records, etc.? _____

SECONDARY FUNCTIONS
Hobbies or special interests?_____
Game table or special furniture? _____

SPECIAL CONSIDERATIONS
Task space, or some decorative wall treatment?_____
Is closet large enough? Can addition be provided?_____

NOTES ON COLOR, MATERIALS, LIGHTING, ETC.
Tile or linoleum floor (watch that chemistry buff)? _____
Special lighting for reading, play, or study? _____
Wallpaper on one wall, cork, supergraphics?_____

OTHER _____
_____
_____
_____
_____
_____
_____
_____
_____
_____
_____
_____
_____
_____
_____
_____

10/ Workroom/ Project Areas

A special workroom or project room is a luxury which will not be available in most budget-designed homes. If you do not have an entire room to spare, a project area is an excellent substitute. Workrooms can be fashioned out of parts of basements, attics, and even large walk-in closets. A workroom cannot accommodate the functions of a workshop, such as major woodworking or automobile repairs—yet it is more than a room with a desk.

Function and organization are the keys to planning and designing workrooms or project areas. In fact, aesthetic considerations are not really important, though a well-organized workroom can be beautiful in its own right.

There are three good ways to design a workroom for little money. One is to do it yourself—build shelves, counters, and storage units out of lumber, plywood, or whatever appropriate material you can handle. The second is to put together a makeshift area with leftover furniture, used furniture, or furnishings found in junk shops. The third, and perhaps the best way, is to use industrial and commercial products. For instance, for storage you can buy some very inexpensive industrial or office steel shelving. You can purchase storage cartons in different colors and stack these on the shelving for a well-organized, color-coded storage system. You can obtain steel tables, or workbench supports to which heavy boards can be bolted as a work surface.

Assembling that kind of table/counter requires few skills and does not cost much. Drafting stools are available in art supply stores. Their advantages are moderate cost and height adjustability. And since a work or project table should probably be higher than a writing table, to allow for working while standing up, an adjustable stool is almost a necessity. Art supply stores are also good sources for drafting tables (which can serve myriad functions other than drafting) and for storage cabinets for small parts and objects such as hardware, string, ribbons, and stationery supplies.

Wall-hung shelves are inexpensive and will hold many tools and supplies. Pegboard, too, will help you organize small tools and miscellaneous objects. Painting the outline of the tools on the board is a graphic and decorative way to help you put them away in the right places. Pegboard (perforated Masonite) can be bought precut and framed, but it is cheaper to purchase a whole sheet in a lumber yard. Most lumber yards will cut the board to whatever dimensions you need. One 4 x 8 sheet should be adequate for your workroom, with several pieces left over for the kitchen or other areas in your home.

The best floor covering for workrooms is a tile surface or a wooden floor. Carpeting is undesirable since almost any activity in a workroom will be messy.

For lighting, a fluorescent fixture would be the most efficient. If, however, your work area is already fitted with incandescent lighting, you may simply want to supplement it with some clamp-on lights. One of the cheapest and most appropriate lights for such a room is a photographer's light, consisting of clamp, socket, and aluminum reflector.

Since the appearance and equipment of workrooms and project areas will vary considerably from case to case, only one possible arrangement is illustrated here.

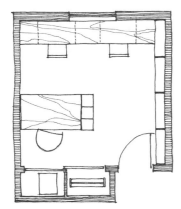 *Plan of workroom shown on page 80.*

A workshop and hobby area has been created, using file cabinets, a simple chest, and a work counter. Steel shelving holds a variety of objects on one wall, and an old wooden office desk and industrial lighting fixtures are further suggestions for inexpensive yet highly functional furnishings.

CHECKLIST Some Recommended Considerations for WORKROOM/PROJECT AREAS

PRIMARY FUNCTIONS—ACTIVITIES
Sewing or weaving? _____

Crafts (jewelry, leatherwork, wood carving)?_____

Photography (would require darkroom and plumbing)? _____

Collecting stamps, coins, rocks, etc.? _____

Painting, sculpture, and other kinds of artwork? _____

SECONDARY FUNCTIONS
Wrapping packages? _____

Ironing? _____

Preparing Christmas cards? _____

Guest room? _____

SPECIAL CONSIDERATIONS
Work counter? _____

Pegboard or cork? _____

NOTES ON COLOR, MATERIALS, LIGHTING, ETC.
Good lighting? _____

Flooring for easy maintenance? _____

OTHER _____
_____
_____
_____
_____
_____
_____
_____
_____
_____
_____
_____

11/Guest Room/ Extra Room

A real guest room is rare in modern homes, and the idea of a formal guest room does not really reflect today's life-style. These brief notes, then, are addressed to those who do have the luxury of that extra space.

Although the best approach might be to spend no funds at all on such a room, still, you will need to think carefully about the design of the guest room. Otherwise it will become a dumping ground for old things, a storage room for empty cartons and old suitcases.

Old furniture, or inherited or borrowed pieces from friends or relatives, will probably be adequate for your guest room. The trick is not to let the room appear to be full of rejects. Better to keep the furnishings to a minimum than to crowd in lots of odds and ends.

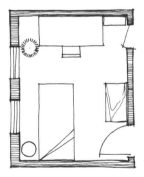

Plan of guest room shown on page 83.

A guest room can also be used as a study. An old oak chest and a box spring and mattress with a printed cotton cover are basic guest furnishings. Desk consists of two file cabinets with a flush door top. Parchment globe light is an inexpensive feature.

One or two beds will certainly be necessary. The section on movable furniture discusses a variety of beds (see p. 140). Probably the least expensive and least bulky bedding would be a "high-rise" bed. An old chest of drawers, stripped and refinished or painted, and some kind of low bedside table would complete the room's real requirements. If there is a closet, 12 inches of hanging space should be more than adequate for guests. The remaining closet space can be used to store extra family clothes or other belongings. If there is no closet in the room, perhaps you should install some brass hooks on the door or behind the door for hanging up clothing.

Often it is practical to combine a guest room and a project room. This can also give the extra room a bit more character and make it seem less like an underfurnished hotel room.

The cheapest way to create interest in an ordinary room is through the use of color. You might experiment in your extra room with a daring color scheme, perhaps painting the whole room in a chocolate brown or other heavy color, or painting one wall in an accent color in contrast to the other walls. Or maybe that is the room where you can try out supergraphics (see section on color, p. 119).

CHECKLIST Some Recommended Considerations for GUEST ROOM / EXTRA ROOM

PRIMARY FUNCTIONS—ACTIVITIES

How often do you anticipate guests? _____

Will they be mostly couples or single friends? _____

Is there a closet? Does it have enough space? _____

If closet has too much space, can it double for your
own use? _____

Does the guest room have some drawers or shelves? _____

SECONDARY FUNCTIONS

Sewing? _____

Projects? _____

Study? _____

SPECIAL CONSIDERATIONS

Table surface or a bedside table? _____

Trundle bed or "high-rise" bed? _____

NOTES ON COLOR, MATERIALS, LIGHTING, ETC.

At least one good reading light? _____

Some feature to differentiate room from a hotel room? _____

OTHER _____

_____
_____
_____
_____
_____
_____
_____
_____
_____
_____
_____

12 / Kitchens

The kitchen is much more than a specialized work area. It is where families like to eat, talk, sit with friends, and gather for just about every kind of activity. Historically, kitchens were literally the heart of the home—the place where the family lived. In the earlier part of this century, many kitchens, especially in city apartments, were designed as minimal functional work spaces, but in recent years homes and even apartments have again been planned with more generous kitchens.

A well-planned kitchen has a compact work area. Large kitchens are hard to cook in if the distance between the major appliances and working area is excessive. Basically, the flow of work proceeds from refrigerator to counter surface to sink to range or oven to serving area. Studies of space/time/motion and human factors have proved several plans to be the most efficient. These are classified as corridor plans, L-shaped plans, and U-shaped plans. Island work spaces for large kitchens and Pullman-type kitchens for very small apartments represent the extreme situations at either end of the scale.

Any modification to work areas should have function as its prime goal. In spite of the fact that American kitchens are famous all over the world, a closer look at these marvels of efficiency reveals many flaws. The standard design of storage facilities makes it very difficult to reach the higher shelves, and the standard ovens force people constantly to bend down to see what's cooking. If you should have the opportunity to plan a new kitchen, my brief comments on kitchen design will not be enough. I strongly recommend that you carefully analyze the needs, human factors, sizes, and clearances involved before settling for the usual plan, appliances, and cabinetry.

If minor modifications are possible, you might refer to the section on built-in kitchen furniture for a few inexpensive improvements (see p. 157). Above all, the addition of some shelving and hanging space (using perforated Masonite) can be a significant improvement for little money.

The breakfast area or eating area may not allow any variations at all; the only decision that might have to be made is what kind of furniture to buy. The typical "dinette" set is usually very poorly designed; there are a number of better alternatives which are both cheaper and more interesting.

Many contemporary, low-cost furniture stores sell simple round or rectangular tables with plastic laminate tops. Or try office furniture stores and showrooms dealing with "commercial" furniture. If you have very little space in your kitchen eating area, a pedestal table from a restaurant supply firm might be the right answer. A kitchen table should be surfaced with a material that can be used for general kitchen work as well; plastic laminates, butcher block, glass, or slate (expensive) are all good materials. Antique shops are excellent sources for old oak tables, which, when stripped down, may make fine tables for eating and working.

Lightweight yet sturdy chairs can be found in low-cost stores. Bentwood chairs, some Italian imports such as the "Chiaviari" type, or country furniture chairs are more comfortable and appropriate than the chrome or wrought-iron ones that come with dinette sets.

As suggested in the section on built-in kitchen furniture, even a small eating counter is worth installing for breakfast or quick snacks. These can be simply made out of Formica-topped slabs or butcher-block tops, and one or two stools can be pushed under the counter when not in use. Simple, very inexpensive stools can be purchased in art supply stores. You can improve a cheap drafting stool with a flat seat cushion or by painting the seat in a bright color.

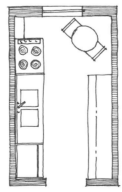

Plan of a small kitchen with round table and two chairs instead of a built-in counter.

In this kitchen, a counter has been added near the window and pegboard has been installed on end walls. Notice the added shelving for jars and spices, as well as plastic bins for fruit and vegetables under part of the counter. This kind of counter works best where there is a deep reveal for the window.

If your kitchen is large, or if it has an adjoining space such as a former pantry, a bit of structural alteration may open up the two rooms into one, and the added space can become a comfortable eating area or even a family room. Or such extra spaces can be converted into laundry and work spaces. If a washing machine or dryer is to be placed directly in the kitchen area, select a front-loading washer, so you can use the tops as additional counter space.

A cart with a practical top can sometimes be used as an extra work surface and for serving, while its lower shelf will store miscellaneous objects. Such carts or "wagons" are available in most major stores; together with a table and chairs, they are often the only furniture additions feasible in completed kitchens.

The best kitchen floors are of quarry, ceramic, or slate tiles, or similar impervious materials such as stone, brick, or terrazzo. None of these are cheap, however; nor can they be installed without major construction work. Should you need kitchen flooring, vinyl asbestos tiles, linoleum, and sheet vinyl with slight textural effects will stand up well. The appearance of a light-colored solid floor is desirable, but without a small texture or pattern (such as marbleized tile), every spot will show. When choosing kitchen flooring, try to avoid the frankly imitative patterns, such as mosaic, flagstone, and brick, that seem to be the norm for cheap linoleum and vinyl sheet materials. Indoor-outdoor carpeting and other special carpets are made for use in kitchens. Although these carpets are very serviceable and sometimes attractive, they do not clean as easily as tile.

The emphasis in kitchen lighting must be on good visibility; fluorescent fixtures are the most efficient. Specific fixtures are mentioned under lighting (p. 170), and that section also recommends the addition of strip lighting under cabinets. A good center fixture is a large globe light—not quite as efficient as fluorescents, but very handsome and giving off good illumination.

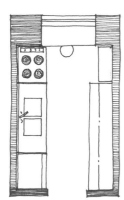

Plan of kitchen shown on page 88.

A butcher-block table teed off the wall containing some built-in shelving and four simple rush bottom chairs make this a very attractive and practical dining area. Notice the movable storage cart/work counter in left foreground.

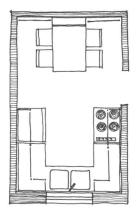

Plan of U-shaped kitchen shown on page 90.

Since visibility is essential in kitchens, light wall colors are best. Painting is cheapest, but kitchens are the one space in homes where the expense of wall covering is really worthwhile. Because of the grease and steam from cooking, kitchens need to be thoroughly washed from time to time; even enamel paint does not stand up too well when frequently scrubbed. Vinyl "wallpaper" (really cloth) is the best surface. For a permanent home, a strong wall covering is a good investment. If you live in temporary quarters, paint or inexpensive paper should be sufficient. Contact papers do not last even a year or two, but they can be used for shelving, for the backs of shelves, and for storage cabinets. They come in a good range of colors and dress up some surfaces that are beyond restoration (though not major wall or ceiling surfaces). Unless you prefer strong colors, colors in the yellow family are cheerful and good in their light-reflecting quality. Most kitchen wall coverings are patterned; I recommend that you not overuse patterns.

If your kitchen cabinets have wood, plastic laminate, or factory-baked enamel finishes, they are probably best left as they are. But for rather ancient wooden cabinets, paint is the cheapest and best solution. Older kitchen cabinets have hinged doors made of frames and inset panels. You might paint the frames and panels and hardware in alternating colors. Cheerful alternating color schemes could also be used on cabinet drawers and drawer fronts.

The decorative possibilities for kitchens are myriad. There is no reason why artwork, posters, or photographs cannot be hung in kitchens. It might be fun to display attractive restaurant menus, or concert or art exhibition announcements, or old maps. An excellent, fitting decorative scheme for kitchens is the display of pots and pans and handsome tools. Well-designed cooking utensils are not cheap, but a few copper pots, new or old, or colorful contemporary pots and pans are nice to use as well as to display. Recommendations for hanging objects on pegboard and suggestions for shelving for both storage and display are detailed in the section on built-in kitchen furniture (p. 157).

If your kitchen is fairly subdued and has the typical kind of apartment-house sterility, colorful curtains might be the right touch. Or if you have enough color already, a bamboo matchstick shade or wooden slat blinds might be better. And more than anything, plants can enhance a kitchen window. What better place for plants than a kitchen, where water is plentiful, and where it is easy to care for them? Incidentally, it is quite simple to grow herbs on window sills or in hanging pots, thus truly combining function and decoration.

CHECKLIST Some Recommended Considerations for
KITCHENS

PRIMARY FUNCTIONS—ACTIVITIES
Can you consider any modifications such as
   New or additional counter space?_____
   New or additional storage space? _____
   Shelving or hanging space? _____
Is there enough room for eating in the kitchen? _____
Do you have counter space for eating? _____

SECONDARY FUNCTIONS
Laundry equipment? _____
Work space? _____
Family room? _____

SPECIAL CONSIDERATIONS
Flooring?_____
Lighting?_____
Painting?_____
Wall covering? _____
Finish of cabinets? _____

NOTES ON COLOR, MATERIALS, LIGHTING, ETC.
Window treatments? _____
Plants?_____
Wall decorations? _____

OTHER _____
_____
_____
_____
_____
_____
_____
_____

13/ Bathrooms

There are two possible approaches to the design of bathrooms: the strictly functional and the luxurious. In many homes bathrooms are limited in size, and our concern with budget more or less eliminates the luxury direction anyway. It does not, however, eliminate some reasonably priced decorative ideas; even a small bathroom can be fun to furnish. The combination of our puritanical heritage with our national pride in American plumbing meant that for many decades the typical apartment bathroom was as small and efficient as possible, often with no amenities beyond the essentials. Not too much can be done with those bathrooms other than a cosmetic face lift. Older buildings, some more recent ones, and those buildings that have been converted from single occupancy often provide somewhat more bathroom space; if you have extra space, there is potential for more interesting design solutions.

The possibilities for major alterations are usually restricted by limited space, but above all by the question of cost. I am assuming here that expensive bathroom remodeling is fairly low on your list of priorities.

If you have extra space, perhaps the creation of some "compartments" for the toilet, possibly an extra shower, or some partitions to define these areas might be a do-it-yourself project. The addition of shelving or closet space for towels and supplies is not as expensive as moving and rearranging plumbing fixtures, and just those minor modifications can make a great improvement. Instead of a prefabricated vanity table, consider making your own. You can order a plastic laminate counter from the lumber yard and have the yard cut out the opening of the sink (this is done by means of a router). You might set the counter between a wall and, for example, a partition. The built-in counter is cheaper than the prefabricated unit, and instead of the often useless undersink storage it might look better to have the counter "float," with the sink and its pipes clearly visible. The plan and sketch show possible changes for a fairly large bathroom.

If your bathroom has ceramic tile floors, it is hard to improve upon that material. Even if the tiles are old, it is worthwile to clean, scrub, and restore them and possibly even attempt to replace a few missing tiles. The great advantage of ceramic floors is their resistance to water damage and their easy maintenance. In old buildings, the tile is usually white; if you wish to introduce color, you can do so quite inexpensively with one or two mats or throw rugs or a bright shower curtain. In newer buildings, the ceramic tiles are usually in colors; since the cost of a new floor is very high, it is probably best to live with what's there even if you don't like it and work around it. Inexpensive high-rise buildings as well as inexpensive private homes and remodeled buildings frequently have bathroom floors of asphalt tile, which costs only a fraction of the price of ceramic tile. It is a serviceable material, and again I would recommend that you live with it rather than try to replace it.

Whatever flooring exists can, of course, be covered with carpeting. Indoor-outdoor carpeting, as well as the more luxurious water- and soil-resistant types, is readily available. It will not cost much to carpet a small bathroom, especially if you are able to cut and fit it yourself. It is not necessary to install bathroom carpeting permanently; in fact, it is a good idea to be able to pick it up from time to time for cleaning purposes. The do-it-yourself bathroom carpeting is made with this in mind.

Sometimes a remnant of cotton carpeting can be bought cheaply and fitted carefully, so that it can be picked up and thrown into a washing machine for cleaning. Of all the possible treatments for floors, the least expensive is to leave the floors alone and simply buy one or two mats for comfort and appearance.

Bathroom walls and ceilings can be painted or covered with paper or vinyl to provide the least expensive personal expression and design. As always, paint is cheapest. Sometimes it might be better not to paint all surfaces with a strong color since that will tend to make the space seem smaller than it is. If

Bathroom with new suspended counter backed and flanked by mirrors. A makeup counter has been added between new storage and end wall. Note suggested lighting and flexible mirror. Tub has been enclosed.

Plan of a fairly large bathroom, such as is frequently found in older houses, showing possible subdivisions and added storage facilities. See page 96.

you have sufficient down-lighting that does not need a white ceiling for reflection, a brightly colored ceiling can be very effective. Perhaps a bathroom is a logical place to experiment with some supergraphics, designs, or stripes (see chapter on color, p. 119). In fact, if you want to try exciting colors, a bathroom is often suitable for such an experiment, since nobody spends very much time in it! It is important, however, to remember that the reflection of color will definitely affect your complexion and appearance. Thus a cool blue or green color will tend to make you look pale or even sickly when reflected in the mirror, whereas a warm color—such as pumpkin or gold—will give you a healthy glow.

Bathroom wallpapers are available in many price ranges and even more designs. Plain paper does not stand up well in a steamy environment and would therefore be false economy. (If you have a half-bathroom, or so-called powder room, plain papers are adequate.) Many papers either come treated with a plastic finish or can be treated with coating by the manufacturer. This option is a service offered by many stores. The most permanent wall coverings are the fabric-backed vinyl papers, but they are more expensive. Unless you own your home, or plan to stay in your apartment for many years, vinyls might not be the most economical choice.

A touch of luxury, which does not have to be costly, can be created with mirrors. In a defined (built-in) area behind the sink, or on one wall surface, a completely mirrored area or wall will add real sparkle to any bathroom and will also serve a useful purpose. Another possible touch of luxury might be the introduction of wood paneling in some areas. But mirrors and wood paneling installed professionally are way out of line with most budgets, so they should be considered only as do-it-yourself projects. Prescored tile panels, adhesive-backed mirrors, and other wall-surfacing materials made for the do-it-yourselfer are frequently of questionable design quality and should be selected with great care.

Many apartment buildings provide the cheapest and ugliest lighting fixtures throughout, and in bathrooms without fail. If there is a ceiling fixture, a simple globe light can be good-looking, efficient, and inexpensive. The more elaborate and expensive special bathroom lights, sometimes made in imitation crystal, are generally fairly pretentious. Shielded (plastic or plexiglass) fluorescent fixtures give off excellent light but are less attractive than globes. If you do use fluorescent lights, be sure to use "warm" or "standard warm" lamps in order to avoid distorted colors. If there is a provision for lighting over or near the sink, a number of reasonably priced fixtures can be found, if the one provided by the building is not simple and acceptable. For a little luxury and fun you might consider lighting strips with small lamps, which are marketed as "makeup" lights and are the kind of lights used in theatrical dressing rooms.

Bathroom hardware and accessories can be extremely costly. Many specialty stores and bathroom boutiques in department stores carry a vast array of expensive, poorly designed gadgets. A much better source, for both price and design, is the hardware stores, especially those that carry architectural hardware (not just household supplies). Towel bars, paper holders, hooks, shelves, soap dishes, and wastebaskets should be selected as examples of good (clean, functional) design; the chances are that your choices will be far cheaper, too, if selected with simplicity and practicality in mind.

Many stores carry matched sets of shower curtains and window curtains, often in the same pattern as matching wallpaper. Again these are somewhat expensive, and not necessarily great design. Many shower curtains have such obvious designs as fish or nautical motifs. Look rather for a good color, a bold geometric design, or perhaps some strongly contrasting stripes. One of the best buys in shower curtains are the plain plastic liners sold for use with elaborate curtains. Sometimes a plain white plastic shower curtain is perfect (these are *really* cheap). Plain window shades, colored window shades, or shades with a laminated pattern are frequently just fine. If you prefer curtains, readymade curtains can be used. Silk happens to be a very good material; it stands up well to steam, and a small pair of silk-content curtains is not very expensive. Another good window treatment might be shutters; they provide ventilation and privacy, are not expensive, and can be painted in any color.

If there is room, it is handy to have a stool, a chair, a clothes hamper, or any surface which can hold clothing or towels. The typical bathroom stools and elaborate hampers, like all other special bathroom merchandise, are high in price and low in design quality. A simple stool or bench can often be found in an antique shop; caned seats are particularly appropriate for bathroom furniture. Or you might try some of the shops specializing in Oriental imports. Many of these stores carry a whole line of inexpensive basket or rattan furniture; they might also carry covered baskets or chests that can be used as hampers. Since basket furniture is woven of individual bamboo strands, it provides perfect ventilation for a clothes hamper. Should you have lots of extra space in your bathroom, there is no reason why you can't introduce some real chairs, a "fun" chair, or a rocking chair.

The final decorative touches do not have to be designed with a particular "bathroom" attitude. Bathrooms can perfectly well have pictures, prints, graphics, or photographs, though perhaps it does not make sense to hang your most valuable or treasured things in the bathroom. Due to the heavy humidity in bathrooms, plants will do well; hang them in a window or place them on a shelf. If there is extra wall space, perhaps on the wall above the toilet, some shelves could be installed. Instead of using the standard bathroom shelves made of glass with metal supports, consider the cheaper wooden shelves installed on wall standards and brackets. If you have extra books or magazines, there is no reason why some of them could not be placed in the bathroom; in fact, many people like to read in the bathroom. (Of course the humidity would not be good for valuable books.)

In summary, I would reiterate that major work in bathrooms is expensive, but that the design possibilities I have suggested can be executed for very little money. I also warn you to stay away from fancy bathroom boutiques and specialty shops. If you approach the bathroom as you would any other space in your home, the result will be better designed, more sophisticated, and inexpensive.

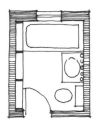

Plan for bathroom shown on page 100.

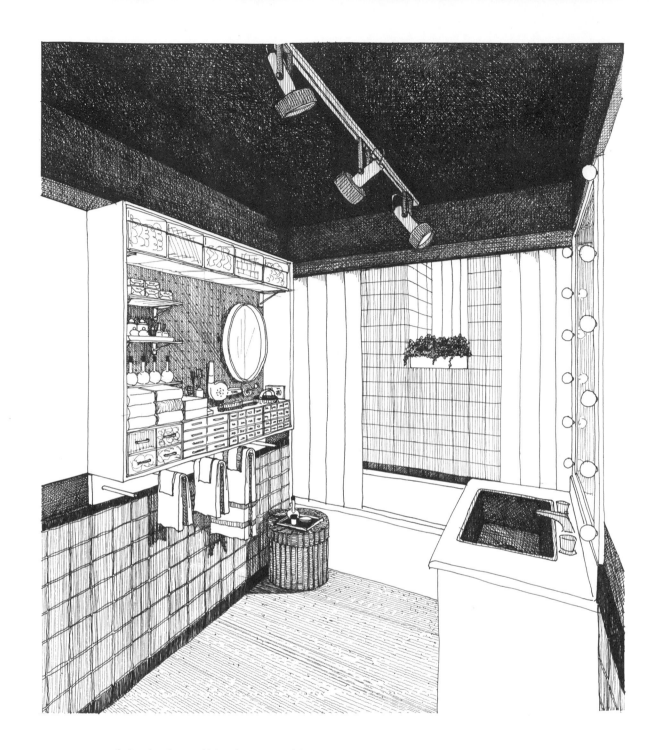

A typical small bathroom with additions: wall-hung shelf unit to accommodate all storage needs, ceiling painted dark, and track lighting plus makeup lights around mirror.

CHECKLIST Some Recommended Considerations for
BATHROOMS

PRIMARY FUNCTIONS—ACTIVITIES
Is there room for a stool, a bench, a hamper?_____
Can shelves or some other storage for towels and supplies
   be introduced? _____
Is there a counter or some other level surface? _____

SECONDARY FUNCTIONS

_____

SPECIAL CONSIDERATIONS
Space for major or minor alterations?_____
Towel hardware, hooks? _____
Are the floors acceptable?_____
Are the walls acceptable? Paint, wallpaper, vinyl?_____
Can anything be done to the ceiling? Paint, paper, vinyl?_____

NOTES ON COLOR, MATERIALS, LIGHTING, ETC.
Can the lighting be improved? _____
Window treatment, if any? _____
Decorations? _____

OTHER _____
_____
_____
_____
_____
_____
_____
_____
_____
_____
_____
_____

14/ Playrooms/ Basement/ Attic

Playrooms are not usually found in apartments. They are, however, a common feature in many houses, usually in basements or in attics. Personally I have some questions about the basic conception of a playroom.

The rapid development of suburbia in the years following World War II gave rise to certain peculiarities. For instance, the "picture window" was an absolute *must*, whether it looked out on a wooded area or on a neighbor's picture window; the split-level house, too, became fashionable—whether or not the scheme made sense for the site or its inhabitants—as did the basement playroom, the family room, or the entertainment room. In many homes the use of the basement or attic room relegated the living room to near-abandonment; or when family activities centered around the living room, the basement or attic rooms were hardly used. While obviously many families, because of their numbers or life-styles, made excellent use of the extra space, other families wound up much like their Victorian forebears with a living room that was in effect a little-used "front parlor." Still other families struggled to pay for houses with playrooms and spent more money to furnish them, only to find that small children played in the kitchen near their mother, that older children wanted the privacy of their own bedrooms, and teen-aged children rejected a specially designated play area.

The basic question I raise if you live in a house with a basement or attic space is: Do you really need that extra room as a playroom, and how will it be used? The question should be asked before you spend money furnishing one. If you have a basement or attic room and decide that you do not need it, it is better to keep it for storage or close it off and invest your efforts and funds elsewhere in the house.

Unless you arrive at a fairly clear program for the basement or attic room, there is a danger that the space will become a hodgepodge full of discarded furnishings and junk. If you plan to have lots of parties, you might need very little furniture in order to provide space for dancing. Consider cushions on the floor, some inexpensive festive lighting such as Japanese lanterns or recessed spots on dimmers, a dark ceiling, and perhaps just one counter or piece of furniture for food and drinks. If, on the other hand, you like to play cards and plan on several games going on simultaneously, then three or four old restaurant tables with bentwood or other inexpensive chairs and good lighting concentrated on the tables might do. If the space is to be used by children, a very flexible open space with some toys and a table might be all that is needed. In that case the furnishings could be as few as those in a play school; perhaps colors or graphics on the walls could provide the design theme for the room. And if the space is to be used as a work space or for some special activity, the approach should be as suggested for workrooms and special project rooms (see p. 78), in which function determines the appearance.

Of all the rooms in a home, the playroom is probably the most suitable one for do-it-yourself projects. Depending on how the room will be used, it might be best to buy as little furniture as possible and construct surfaces, storage elements, or other needed furnishings as suggested in the section on "Classic Makeshifts" (p. 159). While a particular point of view or one strong idea is better than a conglomeration, more than one activity can certainly be planned for the same space. A simple solution can be a storage area created with inexpensive sliding doors or louver doors across one section of the room. This will enable you to store even bulky objects such as a number of card tables.

The prefinished, prescored wood paneling often used to finish playrooms is not really a great-looking material (although I must admit that it is practical). Ordinary sheetrock can be painted in bright colors or decorated with graphics, and it is less expensive than paneling. It does, however, require more long-term maintenance. If a playroom is below grade, dark wood paneling will not do

A basement playroom designed with minimal expense. Seating consists of flush door base with flat cushions. Storage shelves are made of discarded milk crates. End wall is a deep storage closet for bulky toys and extra folding chairs.

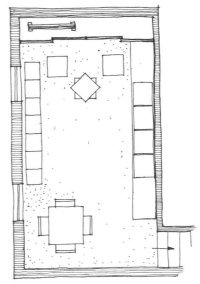

Plan for playroom shown on page 104.

much to lighten it. Similarly, the quality of fluorescent lights, used days and nights if the room is below grade, is not as cheerful and warm as incandescent light. Fluorescent lighting used properly and possibly combined with incandescent lights might be excellent.

The choice of flooring materials is sometimes dictated by existing conditions. For instance, a concrete slab, unexcavated and below grade, is not suitable for wood floors or for every kind of resilient tile floor; asphalt tile or vinyl-asbestos tile is best for such conditions. If no structural limitations exist, flooring depends upon the uses planned for the playroom. Tiles or carpeting, or a combination of these two materials, seems to work best. A good material to consider is carpet tiles, available in indoor-outdoor carpeting as well as the conventional textures and weaves. It is fairly simple to install carpet tiles, and should any problems later arise (water seeping through the floor, for instance, or damage from heavy use), you can repair parts of the flooring without replacing all of it. The price of carpet tiles is quite reasonable. An even less expensive way to carpet a playroom is with carpet remnants and samples. This idea will not appeal to everybody, but it might be fun, especially with children. The combination of different colors and textures will form a huge patchwork quilt. Samples and remnants are very cheap—sometimes even free.

The tighter your budget, the less likely you are to worry about a playroom. But if you do have one, perhaps the ultimate achievement will be to come up with a pleasant and usable space without spending any money at all.

CHECKLIST Some Recommended Considerations for
PLAYROOMS/BASEMENT/ATTIC

PRIMARY FUNCTIONS—ACTIVITIES
What activities are planned for the space? _____
   Parties? _____
   Small children's play? _____
   Projects such as crafts, model railroads, etc.? _____
   Ping-Pong or pool? _____
   Study or work? _____

SECONDARY FUNCTIONS
Guest room? _____
Darkroom? _____

SPECIAL CONSIDERATIONS
Need for storage? _____
Special flooring if space is below grade? _____
Are heating and insulation sufficient? _____

NOTES ON COLOR, MATERIALS, LIGHTING, ETC.
Can one strong design idea be expressed in the room? _____

OTHER _____
_____
_____
_____
_____
_____
_____
_____
_____
_____
_____
_____
_____

15/ Efficiency Units/Studio Apartments

The single-space unit is becoming more and more common in cities. Efficiency apartments can be found in expensive high-rise buildings, with separate dressing areas and many other luxuries. They are frequently found, too, in remodeled row houses or other older buildings. Some come with kitchens, some with small food-preparation areas or kitchenettes within the single living space. The bathroom is often as minimal in size as the apartment itself. Studio and efficiency apartments are meant for one or two persons and are always designed for multipurpose uses. Throughout the previous discussion of room types, I have suggested that assigning more than one function to a room is usually a feasible and economical idea. With efficiency units it is a necessity.

Careful planning for a studio apartment is perhaps more essential than for any other type of home. The smaller the space, the greater the need for intelligent use of every inch.

Some efficiency units feature suggested eating or sleeping areas whose functions could easily be reversed. Any corner or semidefined sleeping area is a real advantage. Whether you live alone or share an apartment, some privacy for the sleeping area may be your most important consideration. Perhaps what your landlord calls a dining space could be separated off as a perfectly adequate bedroom area; thus you would have some privacy if your beds are not made or if your spouse or roommate wants to work while you sleep. If there is no way to designate a special area for sleeping, or if you do not want a separate sleeping area, you might use a bed or beds as part of the living space. A third approach is a convertible sofa, although that has the disadvantage of having to be made up every night.

It is a good idea to consider the sleeping arrangements thoroughly before anything else and to plan the rest of the space accordingly. Because of the

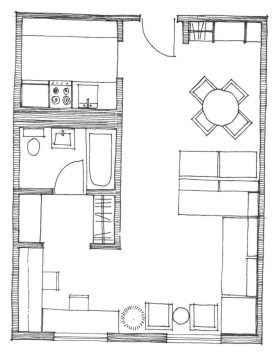

A typical efficiency apartment; here twin beds double as seating in the living area in order to provide work space in the L.

limited size of these apartments, any attempt to create special areas by means of curtains or sliding panels and screens may not succeed. If yours is a plain space, without corners or L-shaped alcoves, some definition can be created with furniture. The back of a sofa (freestanding or teed off from a wall at a right angle) can suggest a division between living space and eating space more subtly than a divider or curtain. A good-sized plant, a freestanding cabinet or table, or any other small-scaled piece of furniture can serve this purpose, too. Two armchairs, side by side, will create a visual division of space between a seating and eating group, or between a seating and sleeping area; in small rooms, such an arrangement tends to create a feeling of space more effectively than the literal introduction of heavy dividers or curtains. One or two chests of drawers or cabinets can serve as dividers, or as headboards for beds, if the backs are finished or covered. It is quite easy to tack plywood or Masonite neatly over the backs of cabinets or chests, and it is much cheaper than purchasing furniture that is made to be completely freestanding.

The need to combine a variety of functions in one space is bound to make one-room apartments rather crowded. Keep this in mind when you select

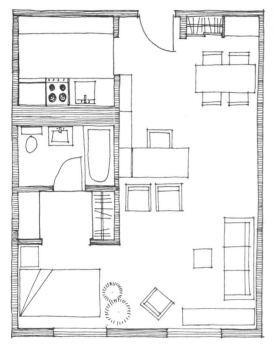

The same apartment, with teed-off desk and two chairs separating living and dining areas.

furnishings. No single piece should be heavy and bulky, and the apartment will be most successful if the furniture is kept light and airy. If you do have a large piece, such as a double bed, it will be wise to make that single item the dominant piece, and attempt to balance the overall distribution of furniture accordingly.

In addition to convertible sofas there are a number of other dual-purpose furnishings, but many are gimmicky and awkward to use. There are coffee tables that can be raised to dining height, armchairs that convert into beds,

Efficiency Units / Studio Apartments / 109

and desks that change into dining tables. It is cheaper, and usually better design, to use your own ingenuity to devise dual-purpose pieces. Instead of buying end tables for a sofa, you might use low chests which provide storage at the same time. Instead of buying night tables for your sleeping alcove, again you can use a chest instead. Instead of buying a console music and television system, you can buy components and place them on shelves or on a low surface. If there is ample space for a dining area, look for dining chairs with arms which can double as chairs around a conversation area for company.

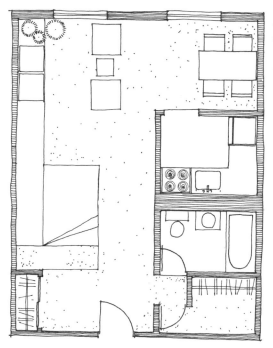

A slightly different efficiency apartment, with a double bed incorporated into the living area. See page 111.

As a rule a dining area should be near the kitchen, but exceptions—such as the case of using a dining alcove for sleeping or as a study—might justify the inconvenience of a dining table somewhat removed from the kitchen. Most studio apartments cannot take a table seating more than four. If you do have room for more than four diners, an extension table or gateleg fold-out table will be a good solution. But if your space is *very* small, a narrow table or counter might be best; when you have friends for dinner, simply serve it buffet-style.

The best way to deal with a large piece of furniture—such as a double bed—in a one-room apartment is to work it into the arrangement rather than try to hide it. Here storage and headboard have been combined in one unit.

Again, if your space is severely limited, and if dining and cooking are very important to you, you might do without a conversational seating group altogether and have instead a fairly large table with comfortable chairs around, which can be used for conversation as well as dining. There is no rule requiring you to have a sofa and standard seating group. A single comfortable reading chair might be all you need.

If you enjoy having company without elaborate meals, the emphasis should be on seating. Any of the groupings suggested under "Living Spaces" (p. 37) and discussed in more detail under the section dealing with furniture (p. 126) can be appropriate. Large pillows on the floor can double as extra seats. And keep in mind that a bed can be very comfortable for seating; with a handsome throw, some bolsters and pillows, even a double bed can be part of a major seating group in a living space.

The plan shown on page 108 shows one solution for a very small apartment using the bedroom area as a study. If you work or study at home, such activities may well be most important to you in planning. A special alcove might hold a conventional desk or a built-in desk (as shown on the plan) and wall-hung bookshelves. Or, depending upon the layout of your efficiency apartment, a study area can be situated near the entry or in the foyer area, or

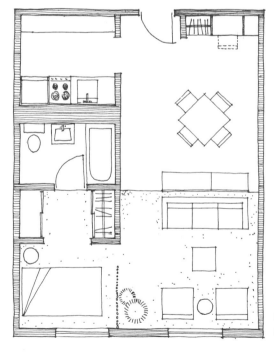

Here the L is used for a sleeping area. See page 113.

This efficiency apartment uses supergraphics as a decorative feature. Planting area in foreground consists of a wooden frame with small stones or pebbles into which several pots have been placed. A hanging screen separates sleeping area from living space.

created by placing a desk backed up against a sofa or a pair of chairs, for example (see p. 109). If desk work is not of primary importance, your dining table can go there.

All these examples point to the need to plan the use and emphasis for a small apartment very carefully. It is a mistake to attempt to condense every feature found in larger homes into a miniature apartment.

Note, too, that there is a measurable difference in planning such an apartment for a single person or for two. Two people will obviously need more storage room. If you already have enough closet space, it might be possible to add some shelving and partitions in the closets for maximum use of that space. If the closet space is inadequate, a storage wall or storage system may have to be devised. If your apartment is in an older building with tall ceilings, consider the possibility, suggested on page 64, of constructing a loft bed. Or if you are not a do-it-yourselfer, there are several readymade or component systems for loft beds on the market. You can increase your available floor space considerably by building a second level or half level for a study area, a reading retreat, or even for storage purposes.

Keep in mind that basically the space is a whole. Colors and textures should reflect the unity of the apartment. Light and airy furnishings, one light color scheme, and one basic design motif are best for a home which consists of a single space.

If your studio apartment is clearly a temporary one, permanent investment does not make sense. Try to live with whatever flooring and basic wall surfacing the building has provided. Forget about wall-to-wall carpeting, unless you are mainly concerned with quick and easy maintenance, and buy an attractive area rug. Rely for the most part on temporary or makeshift furnishings. It is, however, a good idea to buy two or three pieces of furniture: a good armchair, four good dining chairs, or a chest or cabinet will always fit into a more permanent home. If you wait to buy any furnishings until you move to a larger place, your total expenses at that time will be pretty high. Many single people and couples without children prefer to live in relatively small apartments on a permanent basis. If that is your case, your approach to design should reflect this. Even on a limited budget, you should be able to afford a number of well-designed furnishings. A carefully planned efficiency apartment can be extremely attractive and can provide most of the facilities that are normally found in larger places.

CHECKLIST Some Recommended Considerations for
EFFICIENCY UNITS / STUDIO APARTMENTS

PRIMARY FUNCTIONS—ACTIVITIES

What will the apartment's most important function be? _____

    Sleeping—Will you use your apartment mainly as a
              bedroom? _____

    Eating—Will you eat your meals in or out?_____

              Is cooking and feeding friends important? _____

    Entertaining—Will you need lots of seating for
              company? _____

    Work or study—Will you need desk space, bookshelves?_____

    For how many people will the apartment be planned? _____

SECONDARY FUNCTIONS

Overnight guests? _____

SPECIAL CONSIDERATIONS

What special needs? _____

    Music or TV? _____

    Reading or study? _____

    Storage? _____

    Parties or dinners? _____

NOTES ON COLOR, MATERIALS, LIGHTING, ETC.

What special interests might be reflected in the design
    of the apartment? _____

Is easy maintenance a prime concern (wall-to-wall
    carpeting)? _____

OTHER _____

_____

_____

_____

_____

_____

PART THREE

16/ Color

Color is an integral part of every kind of design, not an independent aspect or in any sense an afterthought. It is as much a key element in planning an entire home as in planning a single room.

Color is the quality of light reflected from an object or a surface to the human eye. When light strikes an object, some of its hues are absorbed and others are reflected. The reflected ones give an object or surface its color quality. Certain characteristics are used to describe and define color:

Hue refers to a color's position in the spectrum or in a color wheel. It actually names a color and tells something about its relative warmth or coolness (red and orange are considered warm colors, green and blue are cool colors).

Value indicates the lightness or darkness of a color. White is the lightest value and black the darkest.

Intensity describes the degree of strength and saturation as determined by the quantity of the predominant hue present. It also denotes the degree of purity of a particular color.

The easiest way to understand the position of colors in the spectrum is with a color wheel. The relative positions of colors in a wheel are the determinants for certain standard color combinations and schemes. Therefore, a quick reference to the schematic color wheel will help you understand clearly the terms that are used in discussing color. Red, blue, and yellow are the primary colors; green, violet (or purple), and orange the secondary colors or hues. All the other colors on the wheel are tertiary (or intermediary) colors or hues, such as blue-green, red-orange, and so on. The color wheel is also helpful in understanding what we mean by *monochromatic, analogous,* and *complementary schemes*—terms which are used frequently in discussing color for interiors.

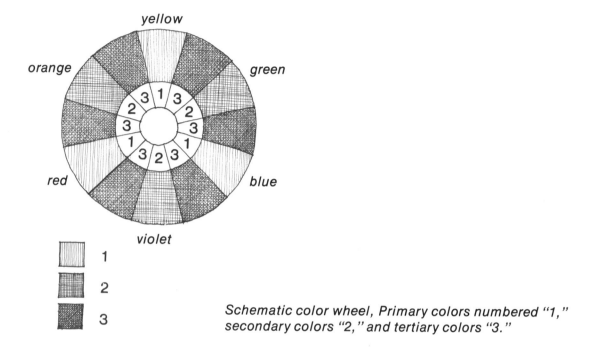

Schematic color wheel, Primary colors numbered "1," secondary colors "2," and tertiary colors "3."

Monochromatic color schemes are based on a single color or hue, varied from dark to light and from almost neutral to full saturation. Monochromatic schemes are perhaps the easiest to handle successfully, especially for those people who do not trust their sense of color. A room with white or off-white walls, one chocolate brown wall, a beige carpet, a tan sofa, and natural-colored linen curtains would be an example of a monochromatic color scheme. In such a room you can certainly use related accent colors, for example, rust-colored chairs, or an unrelated accent color such as blue would be fine. The same monochromatic approach can be taken with greens, yellows, oranges, or any other color.

Analogous colors are adjacent to each other on the color wheel. These colors can successfully be combined. For instance, red, red-orange, and orange are analogous colors; within the context of such a scheme you may well choose to go further toward the yellows, including perhaps yellow-orange and yellow.

Complementary color schemes are based on any two hues directly opposite each other on the color wheel. Be careful here, however. The fact that two colors are "correct" according to basic color theory does not automatically guarantee a successful room. Red and green are complementary colors, but in pure hues they make a Christmas combination, and if used in equal proportion in a room they may be a difficult scheme to live with. One can also use the so-called split-complementary colors, such as violet combined with yellow-orange and yellow-green. Another possible scheme is the double complementary one, which combines two adjacent colors on one side of the color wheel with two adjacent colors on the opposite side.

All these suggested schemes are at best only guidelines. Some beautiful rooms are the very personal expressions of people with a natural flair for color, who totally ignore the conventional rules or combinations. Some of the best decorators have used color schemes that in theory would clash but which work out beautifully in a certain situation. If you feel positive about the use of color, the chances are that you should follow your instinct. If you feel unsure, some of the "approved" schemes or combinations can be helpful, and you might do best to use color rather sparingly. Keep in mind that colors are just one of many aspects of good interior design and that some of the best interiors are basically white rooms with fairly neutral colors.

Many budget-designed homes are quite small; in limited spaces, color should be carefully handled. Warm colors are said to advance, making a space seem smaller, whereas cooler colors tend to recede, making a space seem larger. However, intense hues of either a warm (red, orange) or cool (blue, green) color will give a space a confined feeling. This is why white rooms appear the most spacious. Your choice should be based on whether you want to create a sense of warmth or intimacy or a feeling of openness.

Colors are neither good nor bad; their appropriateness relates to their context. A certain dull or sickly color may be fine in a great painting, but using a color on wall, ceiling, or floor surfaces is quite different from using a touch of it in a painting or fabric. From time to time, popular decorating magazines conduct surveys on the most popular colors, based on which ones sell best in paint, carpeting, or fabrics; it is thus determined that those are the fashionable colors for a particular year. This dictated fashion does not make too much sense, and you should not use the "proper" or "correct" color just because a magazine features it. During the 1950s pastel colors were declared to be "in," while in more recent years strong hues and intense colors have been shown widely in exhibitions and magazines. I personally happen not to like pastel colors. But that does not mean that they cannot be quite beautiful, and many people prefer softly muted colors to clear white.

Color is probably the single subject in this book that does not have a price tag. In other words, materials, fabrics, and certainly paint are not more expensive for being more colorful. Of course, differences in the clarity and richness of colors, especially in fabrics, may mean a difference in price; but by and large color is the cheapest design tool. If you decide on strong-hued paint colors, you may need the landlord's permission or the painter's consent. Many painters are under strict orders by building managements to use only a narrow selection of colors; or they might charge a rather steep price for mixing special colors. If you decide to do the painting yourself, you will find charts and mixing devices in your local paint store which will help you to select from an almost limitless range of choices.

Use your furniture plan when you start to think about color. It might be enough to make notes for each area and upholstery piece, or you might want to try to obtain some samples and fabric cuttings and place them in their appropriate spots on the plan. Start with the large areas: the color of the walls, ceilings, floors, and curtains. If your walls and ceiling will be mostly white, you have a pretty free choice for flooring and fabrics. If you should decide on a very lively carpet, upholstery fabrics must be chosen in keeping with that first decision. A strong-colored floor covering might be enough intense color, and curtains as well as fabrics can then be subdued. If on the other hand your flooring is going to be neutral, you might wish to select some bright or strongly patterned fabrics. When you choose a paint color or a fabric, make sure to look at a good-sized color sample. The larger the area, the more intense the reflective value and appearance of the color.

Many decorating books insist that it is essential to relate all colors in a house or apartment. I don't believe that this should be an absolute rule. If several rooms or areas open onto each other, it generally works well to have some color continuity from one to the other. But if you would enjoy a really different color scheme in a bedroom, or if you want to go all out with an intense color in your bathroom, go ahead. Here are some hints for those who feel a little unsure about color.

- When in doubt, use fewer colors rather than too many.
- White walls and white ceilings give you the most spacious feeling and the most flexible choice for other colors (and also save money on lighting).
- One strong hue or fairly intense color as an accent wall (especially a wall with no doors and windows) can be an exciting and inexpensive color treatment.
- Old furniture can be given a new lease on life with color.
- If you have a really bad ceiling, and especially if the ceiling is fairly high, you may be able to hide all imperfections, pipes, and damage by painting the ceiling a very dark color, even black. If you do, you must be sure to use lighting fixtures with direct downlights (lights not requiring a light ceiling for reflection).
- The easiest color scheme to work with is based on natural and earth colors. Using primarily whites, beiges, neutrals, tans, and browns, you can safely add some touches of rust, orange, or yellow—or just about any other accent color. But a "no color" color scheme is often a fine idea, too.
- Don't worry too much about rules or fashionable color trends. After you have thought through what you like and what you'd like to try, follow your own preferences.

A fairly recent concept combining color and design in bold new ways is called *supergraphics*. Artists and graphic designers have transposed hard-edged painting and studies in fields of color onto the walls of homes and work spaces. Stripes of color run across one wall to another one, or perhaps up onto the ceiling. Squares, circles, just about any two-dimensional shapes, as well as symbols such as arrows, have been used for graphic decorative purposes. Often supergraphics have been used on exterior surfaces of buildings, where numbers and letters become actual design symbols.

There are two ways supergraphics can be handled in interiors. One is to use a wall pretty much as if it were a large canvas by painting stripes, fields of color, patterns, letters, numbers, or symbols on it. The other is to ignore the existing architecture and at times almost consciously to negate or destroy the clarity of the architecture. This means continuing designs across doors, windows, ceilings, and walls, as if no separation existed between planes and surfaces. If you use strong colors and patterns, it will be quite difficult to "read" the space as it was originally designed.

Of course I am wrong when I say that supergraphics are new. Supergraphics in essence are murals, using as their subject matter the nonobjective language of contemporary painting. I stress this fact not just as an explanation of the origins of this "new" idea, but as a warning that it takes a good deal of artistic talent and graphic skill to come up with worthwhile or even acceptable supergraphics. Some people have the talent to go ahead and do it. Others may have to look around carefully for the right ideas, or may be better off seeking the help of an artist or graphic designer.

The medium of supergraphics is especially appropriate for budget-designed interiors. Interesting and colorful graphics will eliminate the need for conventional artwork or for any decorative features or strong colors. Some stores sell large shapes of vinyl plastic with adhesive backing that can be arranged in a number of combinations as do-it-yourself supergraphics. These systems are certainly fun and can help prevent mistakes, but they will cost considerably more than paint.

Examples of supergraphics.

17/ Movable Furniture

The basic forms and proportions of furniture have not changed much over the centuries. Some examples of early Egyptian chairs, for instance, look remarkably similar to the chairs we design and use today. This is because people have not changed very much in size and shape (though we tend to be taller today than 3,000 years ago) and because well-designed furniture obviously must be made to the measure of those who use it. The height of a chair seat, its proportional depth, and the angle of back support must be comfortable for seating. Any storage piece that has shelves higher than 6 feet or that is more than about 20 inches deep is not very convenient. And any table surface much lower than 28 inches is uncomfortable for dining or writing. We can eliminate from the "good design" category anything that is different merely for the sake of being different without serving a purpose.

The following sections devoted to seating, storage, tables, and sleeping will illustrate just a few typical examples of each type. A few words of caution and advice about each category of movable furniture, together with some good examples, should help in making decisions about your own budget-design questions.

Three basic criteria are helpful in evaluating furniture design: the appropriate use of material; the manufacturing process; and the actual form (proportion), detail, and craftsmanship. Craftsmanship in this sense refers to machine-made products and their degree of excellence as well as to traditional handcraftsmanship.

SEATING

The six chairs shown as examples illustrate these criteria. The "Breuer" chair (1) was designed by Marcel Breuer in the 1920s, with chromed steel tubing bent into a continuous shape and fitted with a separate seat and back made of a caned wood frame. This was not only a new idea, but also one which successfully used machine technology and new processes to create a chair that obviously could not be duplicated in wood or any other material. It is a beautifully made and well-proportioned chair, durable and comfortable, using the material in an honest, economical way. Many manufacturers have copied the design, and some have added extra strands of metal and twisted forms for the sake of novelty. All these copies are justifiably unpopular, whereas the original design is still very much in demand today.

The bentwood chair (2) was designed by Michael Thonet over a hundred years ago. It was based on the then-new manufacturing process of steam-bending wood. The design of bentwood furniture is also based on an interesting joint assembly. Instead of the traditional dowels or mortise and tenon glued joints, these chairs are put together with nuts and bolts and screws. When the joints loosen up, the screws or nuts can simply be tightened. As with Breuer's famous chair, there are countless poor copies and copies attempting to create a similar look using other materials.

The wooden chair (3) is a handsome Scandinavian one designed by Hans Wegner which exemplifies sensitive use of wood, fine detail in the grain and in the joints, and just the right dimensions at the critical joints for proper strength. The finish, the selection of beautifully grained wood, and the large amount of handworkmanship make this an expensive chair. But it is also a good example of furniture which does not employ new processes or new materials.

The plastic shell chair (4) is one of many of this type developed recently, based on the new material, plastic, and using molding technique for shaping the seat. By now there are many types of plastic shell chairs—some good, some bad. Many are made for highly specific functions such as stacking or

(5) *sling*

(4) *plastic shell*

(2) Thonet

(1) Breuer

(3) Wegner

(6) *foam*

CLASSIC CHAIRS

ganging and are not really intended for use in the home. But some, certainly the new Italian plastic designs, for example, are definitely suitable for residential use.

The sling chair (5) was a most ingenious design based on an inexpensive combination of wrought iron and canvas. When first introduced (late 1940s), it sold for about $15 in top showrooms and stores. The chair was copied so widely and so badly that many people have rejected it. It is still available in pretty much the original form and price and, although not as comfortable as a large overstuffed chair, it is an excellent buy.

The last chair (6) is an Italian design of foam construction with a stretch fabric cover. It is packed in a vacuum container of plastic and shipped as a flat package. When the seal of the container is broken, the chair slowly opens up, much like a flower, and ultimately holds its comfortable, permanent shape. It is a design very much based on a specific material and process.

Comfort is as important as price and design in choosing the right kind of seating. Since we are not all built exactly alike, it is a good idea to sit for a few minutes in a chair or on a sofa before buying it. And, especially if you spend a lot of time reading, watching television, or listening to music, try to select at least a couple of pieces—armchairs or sofa or two-seater—for real personal comfort.

In small apartments or homes, flexibility is the key. You will want to be able to move dining chairs to your living area or to use a desk chair or bedroom chair for an additional dinner guest. You might find inexpensive and fairly well-designed folding chairs. Stored in a closet, these prevent overcrowding and save a good deal of money as well.

For sofas, the standard 6- or 7-foot sofas are the most reasonable buys. They will fit into any other home without difficulty, which is not always the case with 8-foot or larger sofas (and you won't have to pay the movers extra when it doesn't fit in the elevator!). Some low-cost furniture stores feature two-seaters or loveseats, which are inexpensive and can be particularly appropriate to the scale and proportion of small rooms.

Construction features to look out for in seating:

- In wooden chairs, check the joints, particularly where the back is joined to the seat. A crack in a new chair spells trouble. Sit on the chair to see if it wiggles or creaks when you lean back (and be careful if it does).

- Upholstery details are difficult to check. It is unlikely that any low-cost furniture will have hand-tied coil springs. If, however, this costly method has been used in budget-priced furniture, then it is likely that corners had to be cut elsewhere. Therefore, I would recommend instead "no-sag" type springs, rubberized webbing, and foam seats and pillows.

Fabrics are discussed under that heading in another chapter. Caning and rush seats are durable if properly cared for and are usually very handsome. Obviously these materials make sense only on chairs.

A recent development is the inflatable seating unit. Some are quite attractive, some are great fun, but in spite of their low price they simply do not provide the comfort of other types of seating. They can also be hot during the summer and not particularly pleasant to the touch. Some inflatable furniture is really well designed in terms of form, material, and manufacturing process, but it usually lacks the important elements of comfort and satisfaction to the user.

(*Opposite*)
WELL-DESIGNED, INEXPENSIVE CHAIRS (*1*) *A simple wooden "country" chair with rush seating. This chair has been made in many regions for years. It is often available unfinished and is always rather inexpensive. (2) A very well-designed folding chair; it is handsome enough to be used for dining or as a desk chair, and it is one of the least expensive. (3) Similar to the chair shown on the far left, this is a "country"-style wooden dining chair with rush seating. Because of its height and arms it is somewhat more expensive than the chair at left, but it is still a most reasonable buy. (4) A traditional design originating in Italy. Sometimes sold under the name "Chiaviari" chair, it is delicate yet quite sturdy. Seats are natural rush or nylon cord. Most often it comes in black lacquer, but it is sometimes marketed in white or other colors. (5) "Director's" chair; a classic design with canvas seat and back. Chair folds for storage and is handsome enough to be used in almost any setting. Because it is mass-produced, it is extremely reasonable. (6) A simple plastic or fiber glass stacking chair. These mass-produced chairs are most frequently used in institutional settings. However, the design of the chair is very good, and it makes an excellent, inexpensive dining or work chair.*

(1)

(2)

(3)

(4)

(5)

(6)

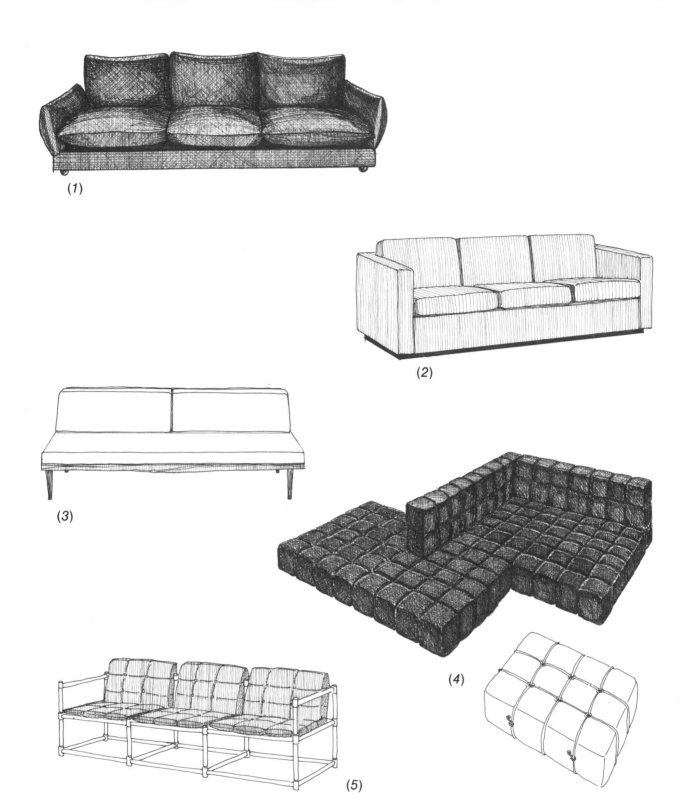

(1)

(2)

(3)

(4)

(5)

STORAGE

In former days, a bride's dowry usually included a bulky set of bedroom furniture, a large armoire, a breakfront, or a big hutch. Since we are now a rather mobile society, we have to consider the difficulties of moving monumental pieces of furniture. And today most apartments and houses have built-in closets. For our purposes then, smaller, lighter-weight, and perhaps modular storage units are a much better investment.

Well-designed contemporary storage units are suitable for bedrooms, living rooms, or any other spaces in a home. Perhaps you need only a couple of chests for bedroom storage. But it would be wise to buy so that in another home more units can be added, or so that these units could form the beginning of a complete storage wall. I have mentioned that unpainted cabinets are often well designed and inexpensive (see p. 68). Some of the major national mail-order companies also carry storage units. Many low-cost retail furniture shops specialize in inexpensive storage cabinets and chests of drawers, often available in a number of choices of veneer and finish. A word of warning about any "bargain" storage cabinets: be sure to measure the depth. Often the standard depth of 18 to 20 inches has been reduced to 15 or 16 inches in order to economize. The drawers in a shallow chest are then too small to accommodate standard items such as folded shirts (approximately 14 x 8 inches folded).

Chests of drawers are more expensive than cabinets with sliding or hinged doors. The cabinet with doors has an advantage over the chest of drawers—it

(*Opposite*)
WELL-DESIGNED, INEXPENSIVE SOFAS (*1*) *A sofa or two-seater usually covered in denim with soft, shredded foam or polyester stuffing. Handsome, comfortable, and inexpensive, but not made to last forever.* (*2*) *A "classic" tailored sofa that comes in many price ranges. The most reasonably priced ones may not have expensive hand detailing such as welting or tufting, but the simple form is timeless and good-looking.* (*3*) *Probably the least expensive type of sofa marketed. Many stores specializing in foam rubber carry these sofas. Lightly scaled for small spaces, they also can be used as an extra bed by removing the back bolsters.* (*4*) *Example of "modular" seating units that can be arranged as sofas, as seating environments, or singly as ottomans.* (*5*) *A very inexpensive seating unit. Not as soft as a fully upholstered sofa. Marketed in parts, to be assembled by owners, and very appropriate for temporary settings.*

Examples of simple, inexpensive storage cabinets.

can be used for dishes, papers, bottles, or just about anything else when moved out of the bedroom to another area.

For determining the quality of a storage unit, drawers are the key. The way a drawer is made (dovetailed, grooved, nailed) determines its durability; the way it is fitted determines its proper operation. Even in well-made old chests, the drawers and the drawer bottoms often need repairs. This is because a movable part in a piece of furniture takes much more abuse than the rest. The new plastic drawers have overcome that problem: they are molded in one piece. If you can find plastic drawers at a reasonable price, consider them. If you want to economize and avoid problems, use as few drawers as possible.

For storing papers, files, and magazines, file cabinets are an often-ignored possibility. They are "classic makeshift" storage components for work spaces and can be used as desk pedestals. Stores sell file cabinets scaled down to residential use, and sometimes used file cabinets are really cheap; painting the front can make a file a perfectly good piece of furniture for a bedroom or family room.

A number of excellent "storage systems" are available. The better ones are not really cheap, but they always come in components and open stock and can thus be purchased over a number of years. These systems contain cabinets, chests of drawers, desk tops or units, bookshelves, and compartments for audio equipment. In general they provide the utmost choice and flexibility. However, once mounted on a wall, they are no longer easily movable. Some further examples of these systems are described in the section on built-in storage (see p. 151).

When selecting storage units, pay particular attention to the surface finishes of the tops. A cabinet or chest with a plastic laminate top might be more expensive but worth the investment in terms of maintenance. If you prefer the more luxurious wooden cabinets and tops, try to select a practical easy-care finish such as an oiled finish.

Storage units with fake moldings, plastic carving, or gaudy trim or hardware are poor design, regardless of cost. The examples here are simple, perhaps understated pieces of furniture, which represent good design at reasonable cost.

SURFACES (TABLES)

Every home needs some tables or surfaces in addition to a dining table. Although the conventional labels *coffee table, end table,* and *occasional table* don't make much sense to me, they will have to do for identification. For our purposes, a large, formal coffee table and a set of matched end tables are unnecessary. A practical alternative is stack tables, or a nest of tables. Some of the best and cheapest designs are Scandinavian. The advantage of stack tables is that they are flexible: two can be placed on either side of a sofa or chair, and one or two in front of a sofa or in front of a chair, however needed. Large coffee tables also block access to the center portion of a sofa. For that reason, two small tables in front of a sofa are often more functional as well as cheaper.

Another possibility is the "cube" table, made out of wood, plastic, or glass (the last is expensive). These cubes (usually 14, 15, or 16 inches cubed) are large enough to hold ashtrays, glasses, etc., but do not clutter up limited spaces.

Instead of traditional end tables, consider an elongated table or bench beside a sofa. The space right next to the sofa can hold a lamp, ashtray, and so on; the extension of the surface can be used for audio equipment, for displaying of objects, for plants, for books or magazines. And the surface will give the sofa-plus-table setting a built-in continuous look. The surface can be a simple bench or a makeshift table made of a top (plywood, flush door, old wood) with legs purchased in a hardware store, simply attached with screws.

Another practical end table is a low chest or trunk which can provide hidden storage as well. An old "decorator" trick is a cheap or battered round table covered with a cloth, tablecloth, or felt down to the floor. This was a favorite Victorian treatment, but it can work quite well in contemporary settings. Some of these arrangements are more interesting than standard tables and are certainly cheaper.

Of the "real" coffee tables and end tables available in stores, several examples are shown. Steel (or polished aluminum) and glass are usually quite elegant if simply made, without superfluous parts and decorations. Shopping around for reasonable buys in these handsome tables may take some time and effort, but will usually pay.

Parsons tables come in all sizes and shapes, from dining height to coffee

Examples of simple, attractive low tables.

table height. The design quality of these "classics" depends largely upon good proportion. Those made in plastic laminates (such as Formica) are very durable.

Naturally, you should choose surface materials carefully. Glass can be cleaned with ease, but heavy plate glass is expensive. Thin glass does not look quite as good and breaks too easily. Plastic laminates, oil-finished wood, specially treated wood surfaces (some are alcohol resistant, burn resistant, etc.), and certain patented composition materials stand up well. Slate, marble, and other esoteric table tops are expensive. However, travertine, a kind of marble, is reasonable and rather handsome. A piece of plywood, four square tubing metal legs from a hardware store, and a piece of travertine can give you a good-looking table without very much work involved. One of the most durable and attractive surfaces is butcher block—a wooden surface made of laminated strips of hardwood. Its weight and cost are high, but for counter surfaces, work surfaces, and even eating surfaces it is a very good material.

I have said little about dining tables, since they are discussed in the section on eating spaces. Also, many of the ideas suggested for work surfaces—such as the glass table, opposite—will also do for dining tables.

Desks are both surfaces and storage. For home use, a work surface is usually more important than a desk with drawers and file compartments. If you need a real desk, and if you have enough space, the best buys as a rule are office desks. Second-hand desks can be a real bargain, and the desks carried in office furniture stores can be reasonable buys. For a desk used for household purposes only, a writing table with shallow drawers might be enough. Campaign desks are quite handsome, and some simple Scandinavian teakwood desks are available at bargain prices (usually quite well designed). For more serious desk needs, see the section on "Built-in Furniture" (p. 147).

For children, particularly teen-agers, you might consider modular furniture consisting of cabinets, chests of drawers, and desk-top attachments. These sturdy units are often made with Formica tops. Whether a small desk is needed for your child's room or for your own needs, it may be cheapest and best to plan for such modular systems. In the long run, instead of a collection of slightly different shapes and dimensions, you will have a highly functional, continuous system of modular units.

Work surfaces need not be conventional heavy desks. This writing table on trestle supports is adequate for most home needs—less costly than a "real" desk and much lighter in appearance. The small desk with drop leaf is a Scandinavian design, usually very inexpensive, yet quite adequate as a work surface when drop leaf is raised. The glass work surface is shown on metal trestles—more expensive than wooden supports.

Movable Furniture / 139

SLEEPING FURNITURE

Standard beds are discussed in the section on sleeping spaces, but many households need additional beds for guest rooms, family rooms, and children's rooms. Often these beds must serve more than one purpose.

The most common type, very convenient and advertised widely, are convertible sofas. Unfortunately, the nature of the mechanism makes these sofa-beds look bulky and heavy. A convertible sofa with good lines and good proportions will not be cheap.

If you plan to buy a sofa and need an extra sleeping space only infrequently, the least expensive solution is a sofa with removable back bolsters. If you have extra closet space, a folding cot (the roll-away type) can provide that extra bed when needed. However, folding cots are made as single beds only; convertible sofas come in every size up to king size, so they would be the solution if you have couples visiting frequently.

During the 1920s, a patented foldaway bed called the "Murphy bed" was very popular. Murphy beds are still available, and for those who are handy, they might be a worthwhile consideration. Murphy beds are attached to walls or inside special closets on a hinge mechanism, which makes it easy to fold a bed flat against the wall or into the enclosure during the day. Trundle beds are available, too, often in shops specializing in children's furniture. Some of the European imports are particularly well designed and well made, and are in the medium-price range. The better trundle beds do well as daybeds or sofas, and the lower bed, when pulled out, is identical in size and comfort to the upper one. Some trundle beds are made to stack up in a bunk bed. A bunk bed for children can later be converted to individual beds or trundle beds, justifying the somewhat higher initial price. A very inexpensive trundle bed is the "high-rise" type, consisting of two metal frames with springs and mattresses.

(Opposite)
The platform bed with simple headboard has a more graceful appearance than a box spring and mattress and is particularly appropriate where sleeping areas are combined with other uses. The "campaign" or "Captain's" bed provides extra storage and can be useful for children's or guest rooms. The Oriental rattan headboard is one example in a wide selection available—an inexpensive, decorative idea.

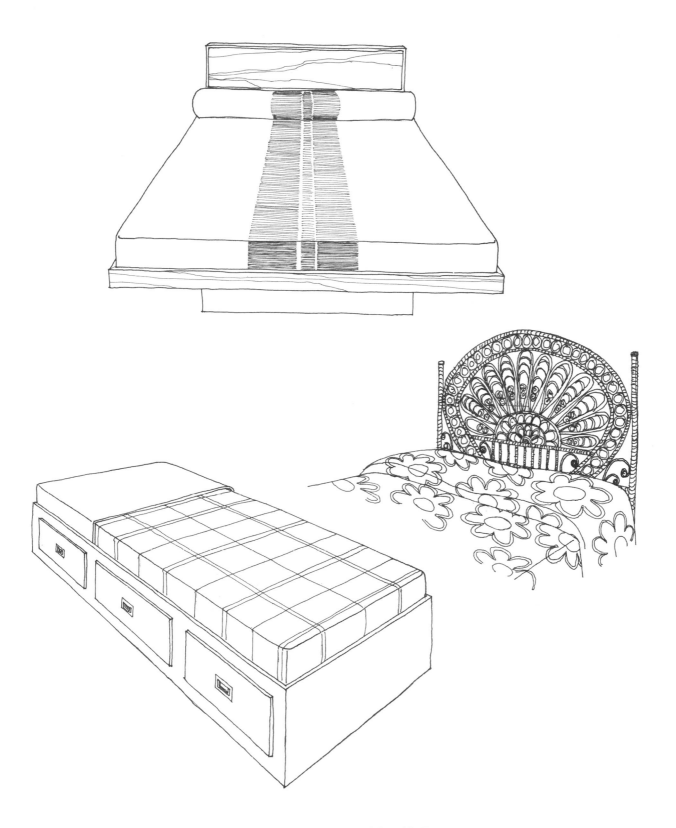

The high-riser, usually somewhat narrower than the average bed, can be made up as a daybed/sofa with an inexpensive throw and is a sensible and flexible sleeping facility for two. If you have limited storage, consider a bed with drawer space below the mattress. A number of these beds are marketed under the name of *campaign* or *Captain's* beds. The drawers are bulky and rather difficult to operate; however, they are not intended to be used often, but rather for extra storage of blankets and bedding, or perhaps for bulky toys.

18/ Built-in Furniture

Custom-built or *built-in* furniture can mean expensive and luxurious installations when a home is professionally designed and if custom work is done by a fine cabinetmaker. The built-in features that are suggested here are do-it-yourself projects, simple projects for a local contractor or handyman, or modifications of store-bought components.

Removable component parts are the most practical if your present home is a temporary one. However, if you need a large number of cabinets, bookshelves, and places for special storage, the cost of buying each item separately might make a built-in unit comparatively inexpensive. Some of the suggestions in the following pages are actually money-saving devices; building storage facilities into an existing closet, for instance, can eliminate the need for an extra chest of drawers.

CLOSETS

Some space-saving suggestions were illustrated on page 70 when we discussed bedrooms. Almost any closet can be made more efficient. Perhaps there is enough height to add another shelf or enough width for an upright plywood divider to form extra shelving space. If you plan to adapt an existing closet to

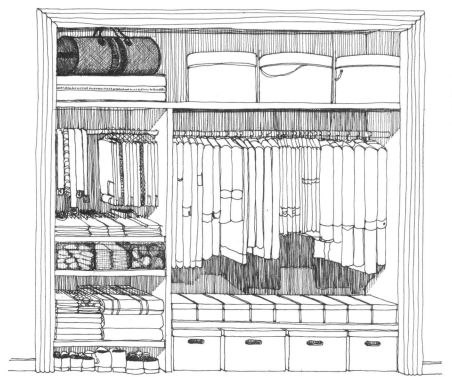

A typical closet with added plywood divider for shelving, and movable storage boxes.

store handbags, shoes, sweaters, and other items, be sure to measure for the exact dimensions to hold these items. Hardware stores sell a variety of devices to hold neckties, shoes, or hats that can be incorporated into your plan. Closets in family rooms or guest rooms can house such major household objects as audio equipment or television sets. A closet can also be fitted with shelves and used as a bar. To convert an ordinary clothes closet into a built-in storage wall, you might remove the door and substitute a pair of louver, panel, or bifold doors. However, it is possible to create a unit that is good-looking enough to be left exposed, with no door at all.

Perhaps you have a single closet built into a room, bulky and ugly, and looking rather like an upended box stuck in a corner. If you do, you might build an identical closet at the opposite corner and use the space between as a real design feature. The leftover space might be used as a headboard area for a bed, providing a kind of canopy setting. Or you might use this space for a built-in desk or storage surface. Your desk or storage arrangement will appear cohesive if you build to the same depth as that of the existing closet. An overhead valance for lighting would be an additional unifying element.

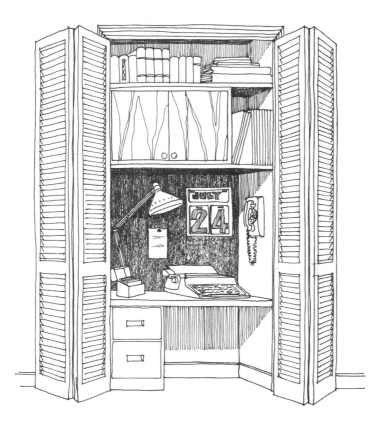

(*Above*) *A closet built out for storage and work space, with louver doors substituted for the original one. (Below) A clothes closet converted into a storage wall with original doors removed.*

In older buildings, closet doors are often eyesores—awkwardly placed, sometimes ugly and worn. One solution is to cover an old door with plywood or Masonite, and then paint it. That surface can also be covered with cork to make a bulletin board, or covered with a luxurious floor-length mirror.

Decorating the inside of a closet can be expensive if wallpaper or fabric is used. The cheapest way to fix up a closet is to paint it; and since the doors will be closed most of the time, have no qualms about using bright and intense colors for fun. It's usually worth a little extra money to install a light. If there is an outlet near the closet, it is easy to run an electric line into the closet and install a simple fixture. Battery-operated closet lights are also available, ready for simple installation.

Desk and extra storage built between closet and wall to create a cohesive unit.

SHELVING/DESKS/WORK SURFACES

The single most suitable, practical, and economical item for building into even temporary quarters is the wall-hung shelf. Everybody needs shelving for books, records, toys, and countless other items. There are a variety of inexpensive standards and brackets which can be attached directly to walls; they are available in hardware and department stores and at lumber yards. If you have never done it before, you might want to get some help, but it is really quite easy to install these standards. In an older building, you can usually simply locate the studs and attach the standards with long wood screws. If the wall is of block construction, plaster, or brick, you will need a masonry drill in order to use toggle bolts, or you can insert lead plugs into a hole and then use ordinary screws. Standards should be no more than 24 inches apart. Properly installed, wall-hung shelves will support the heaviest books safely. In some buildings, permission for this sort of installation must be obtained from the landlord; but it is easy to patch up the screw holes after removing the standards. Of course, since these standards and shelves are reusable, the investment is in time for installation rather than money.

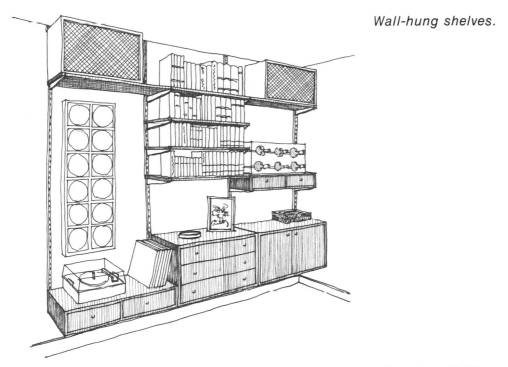

Wall-hung shelves.

Built-in Furniture / 147

Stores specializing in shelving carry the shelves in a variety of wood veneers or surfaced with plastic laminates (Formica or Micarta). The least expensive shelves are those that you can make yourself or purchase in lumber yards (most yards will cut sheets of plywood for you). One sheet of 4 x 8-foot plywood cut into 8-inch strips (adequate depth for normal books) will give you 48 feet of shelving. You can also buy solid shelving in pine or fir or any other wood and finish it to your taste. Plywood shelves may be left natural or may be painted. If the surfaces of any wooden shelves are marred or splintered, you may even wish to wrap the shelves in contact paper.

A somewhat more complicated design will provide a truly built-in, architectural look. This consists of a series of floor-to-ceiling upright wooden members (or fins), fitted neatly from wall-to-wall and floor-to-ceiling, with some fixed and many adjustable shelves in between. Such a unit requires a fair amount of craftsmanship, but it can be done inexpensively using either plywood or solid wood. If an entire wall is designed with built-in shelves, the shelves can be painted the color of the room, painted in a contrasting color, or left natural. Note the suggested details on the drawing. The adjustable shelves can be made to rest on shelf pins which fit into 1/4-inch holes drilled into the wooden sides at regular intervals. The example shown here can be adapted to any other dimension, as long as the spacing between the fins does not become too long. Shelves solidly loaded with books will sag if they are more than 36 inches long.

Built-in storage wall.

Storage wall with teed-off desk.

The bookshelf/library wall can also be a good location for a desk. If there is enough space, one edge of the desk surface can rest at right angles on one of the fixed shelves. This arrangement provides ready access from the desk to reference books, as well as space for files, boxes, telephone, and so on, within the framework of the shelves. A good depth for a desk is about 30 inches, so the upright fins should be spaced about 30 inches apart overall. Since comfortable desk height is generally 29 1/2 inches, the fixed shelf should be placed so that the desk surface resting on top of it will reach approximately 29 1/2 inches. A desk surface teed off from a set of bookshelves can be anywhere from 42 to 60 inches long, depending upon your needs and space. The free end of the desk can be supported by a file cabinet, a drawer pedestal or cabinet, or simply by a sawhorse. The desk top can be a flush door, plywood, or any other material; a Formica-surfaced top is probably the most serviceable.

In the section on room types, I have recommended built-in desks or work surfaces and mentioned some possible designs. A built-in desk or general work surface is ideal for spaces where a wall or a large portion of a wall is used for work, books, projects, and study. A homemade desk is usually much cheaper than a store-bought one, and it can accommodate all kinds of special needs (space for pencil sharpeners, lighting, more than one activity or person, etc.).

In any recessed space, such as between a closet and a wall, one end of the desk can be supported on a wall on a cleat (wooden strip fastened to wall). By far the easiest construction is to rest the desk top on two file cabinets, or on one file cabinet and a cabinet or chest of drawers at the other end. Again, the total height of the desk should be approximately 29 1/2 inches at the top surface. (For children, either use adjustable drafting stools or put the work surface on lower cabinets.)

Probably the least expensive desk surface is a flush door. Even though these doors are hollow, they are quite sturdy enough for normal work. A 7-foot door costs considerably less than that much plywood and requires little trimming or finishing. In fact, you can sand the edges and use linseed oil or wax as a finish. Plastic laminates, paint, lacquer, or even a veneered top in a fine wood can give your flush door or plywood a beautiful surface. Sheet

Flush door desk supported on cleat and file cabinet.

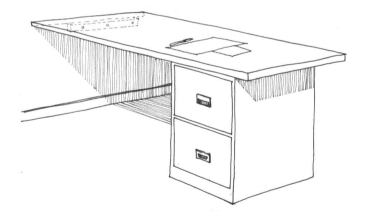

linoleum in solid colors is also a good choice. (Note that a light color such as off-white, gray, or beige provides the best light-reflecting surface.) Sometimes a leftover piece of such heavy-duty linoleum can be bought cheaply in a flooring supply store and can be glued to a wood surface with ordinary linoleum paste. Another good surface material is "chipboard," a sheet material available in the standard dimensions of plywood, made of wood chips rolled into solid sheets with a bonding agent. These boards have dimensional stability, are sturdy and wear well, and have an attractive texture.

STORAGE

Building custom storage walls or units is too expensive for most limited budgets and requires thorough skills. The following suggestions are geared so that your carpenter or cabinetmaker can build custom units that are at least no higher in cost than commercial ones. The important question for you is whether a built-in storage unit is really necessary for functional or aesthetic reasons.

If you do decide to build your own, the best approach is to design and construct units along the lines of the bookshelves described in the previous section. The shelves were described and pictured as *modular units*: they were referred to as a *system*. I shall continue to use these terms for a specific reason.

Almost any furniture design—and indeed any architectural design— is based on a geometric, repetitive, and orderly system. In any successful building, old or new, the spacing of columns, the placement of windows and all other building components are logical; even buildings which look irregular have an underlying geometric system. In good furniture design, we can always detect the same sense of organization. A storage unit or wall stores a variety of objects. The temptation is artfully to arrange shapes and forms for specific items, but such an arbitrary composition will usually be far less successful than one based on a general design principle.

The storage unit typically houses a television, a music system, speakers, records or tapes, books, sometimes a bar or liquor cabinet, bulky items such as projectors, and an array of personal belongings. The fact that television sets, especially color sets, are quite bulky and probably require a depth of 26 inches, while books require a shelf no more than 8 to 12 inches deep, creates a difficulty. That is where the system comes in.

If you plan a unit divided into 24- to 30-inch-wide compartments or modules (very much like the bookcases), almost anything will fit in it. To overcome the differences in depth, consider these two approaches. Use uprights or fins which are from 12 to 18 inches deep; keep the shelving at 12 inches or less, and project the individual cabinets or cases forward to the required depth. Or, concentrate the bulky objects on the lower level, creating the effect of a counter about 32 to 36 inches high, and then place the shallower objects, such as books and records, on a stepped-back upper compartment. This latter arrangement will look somewhat like a hutch or kitchen cabinet, which does not mean that it cannot be well designed and well proportioned. However, I believe that the first approach is better, and the sketch below explains how to achieve it. Many stores selling furniture parts or furniture components also sell cabinets without legs that have hinged doors, drop doors, or sliding doors. Even desk tops or desk units with drop doors are available that way. You might purchase these major units first, then build a

Storage wall with dropleaf desk space.

*Storage wall with
deeper base cabinets
between "fins."*

whole system around them, setting the supporting sides or fins to clasp the cases firmly. The cabinets can simply be attached to uprights with wood screws. The sketches also show how storage units can incorporate desks. Of course, a 30-inch desk set into a unit against a wall is not as convenient a work surface as a larger top, but it might be quite adequate for doing normal household accounts and for letter writing.

A number of manufacturers make storage units based on small, individual components, starting out with simple boxes or cubes. If you measure the available space carefully, you may be able to form a complete "built-in" system with these, stacking them along the length of the wall. Many of these systems include closed cabinetry for a variety of uses.

Most modern amplifiers, turntables, speakers, and tuners are handsome enough to be kept on open shelves. (Furthermore, they function much better when air can circulate freely around them.) Small television sets, too, are usually well designed. Bulky color television sets, though, are a problem. An ideal solution would be to be able to cut an opening into the wall behind the storage unit to accommodate the picture tube, eliminating the need for excessive depth in the storage unit itself—but this is unlikely! If a bulky television set cannot be incorporated into a storage wall, keep it on a stand or cart, or set it on top of a cabinet or chest where a small projection over front and rear edge will not show much.

Remember that the expense of custom-built storage walls might make it worthwhile to seek professional advice from a designer.

SPECIAL FEATURES

For anyone living in old buildings, radiators can be a problem. Though basically not offensive, they can be unsightly (especially when coated with peeling paint) and frequently very hot, so that an enclosure might be a real improvement. Commercially sold radiator covers are rather clumsy and ugly.

The simple radiator enclosure shown in the sketch below is made of plywood or solid boards and painted. Good-quality plywood or lumbercore

Radiator cover incorporated into window wall unit.

can be finished in natural wood finishes. A frame is made of wood and covered with a linen or other loosely woven fabric to permit heat to penetrate. It is easy to cover a frame by wrapping fabric over its edges and stapling it to the back. Leave space between the radiator cover and frame as indicated to permit proper air convection from the radiator. The frame can simply be hung on a couple of screw eyes with wire or with curtain hooks. That way it can be removed for cleaning or for access to the radiator. If the radiator and the area around it are ugly, everything behind the hanging screen can be painted dark gray or black for camouflage.

Radiators under a window sill might be covered and combined with bookshelves from wall to wall. This also provides an excellent surface right under the window for plants or other things. If you are willing to spend more money, consider a washable top made of Formica. The top and the shelves should be wider than the radiator by about 2 inches in order to accommodate the hanging frame. If the unit is over 12 inches deep, the shelves will be deep enough for audio equipment. And if the location seems right, stereo speakers can be set into the shelves adjoining the radiator.

It may be necessary to provide openings in the top over the radiator area for proper heat convection. This can be done by routing out a rectangular opening and inserting a piece of metal grille; or drill evenly spaced 1/2-inch holes over a rectangular area approximately the size of the radiator. Radiators are located under windows to let the rising hot air be set into circulation by the cooler air coming through the window panes. If your rooms are too cool, you will certainly need some kind of opening in the top of your radiator covers.

A single shelf can be an inexpensive and effective design element. For instance in a dining room, a single shelf floating across a whole wall can act as a server, as display space, and perhaps as the only piece of furniture other than the table and chairs. And a small floating shelf in an entry area or foyer can be useful for handbags, mail, and so on.

If a shelf is to go from wall to wall, it can be installed on cleats at each end, with a long strip of wood (cleat) all the way against the back wall. These

Built-in console shelf.

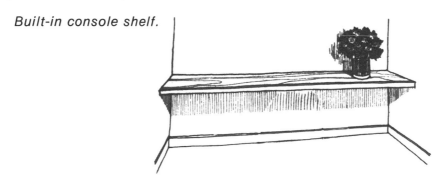

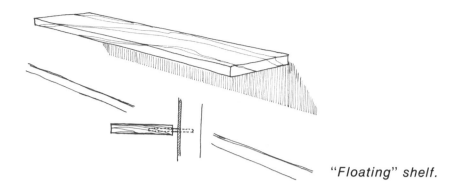

"Floating" shelf.

console shelves should be thicker than bookshelves. A 1 1/2-inch neatly planed and trimmed piece of straight wood would be a good size. Of course you can double two pieces of 3/4-inch plywood, edge the front, and get the same effect. A second method is to support a shelf with angle brackets. The very cheap builders' variety of angle supports, while not particularly beautiful, are probably stronger than some of the ornate scroll types. A diligent search might unearth some simple angle supports or some decorative antique ones. If the angle supports are securely fastened into studs, the free-floating shelf console can support considerable weight; in fact, a plywood shelf may even hold a slab of marble or slate. The third way of supporting a shelf requires a solid wood, preferably hardwood. By drilling a 3/8- or 1/2-inch hole into the wall and into the shelf and forcing a metal rod of the same dimension into the holes, the shelf can actually be made to "float" away from the wall by 1/2 or 3/4 inch. This rather tricky and sophisticated installation does not support a great deal of weight, but it is not as difficult to make as it sounds.

Since I mention floating shelves, I should also point out that many cabinets can be wall-hung, creating an airy and interesting look. Some cabinets, specifically constructed to be wall-mounted, have heavy backs and fastening strips. Many cabinets that have strong plywood backs can be reinforced with

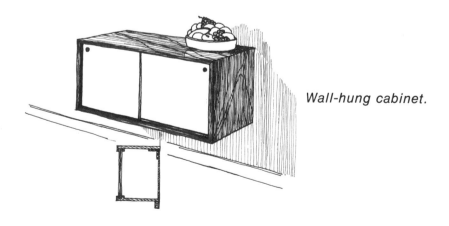

Wall-hung cabinet.

additional wood screws through the back, perhaps a few angle irons inside the cabinet or a heavy strip of wood, and a further strip of wood underneath the cabinet, securely fastened to the wall. Unless you are experienced in carpentry, it would be wise to get some expert advice before doing this.

KITCHEN BUILT-INS

There are a number of built-in features that can be added to a kitchen at little cost and to great advantage.

Pegboard or perforated Masonite is a frequently employed, useful, and decorative device. As I mentioned when discussing workrooms, buying a whole sheet in a lumber yard and getting it cut to size there is better than buying precut and framed pegboards. In most kitchens there is usually space between upper cabinets and counters, on small portions of end walls, between doors, on leftover wall spaces, or even on the back of a door. Pegboard can provide extra hanging and display space for kitchen utensils and pots and pans. Pegboard must be installed on furring strips to provide space behind the surface so that the hooks can be inserted. Among the large variety of pegboard hardware available are hooks of different sizes, brackets for shelves, and special hardware for such objects as spice containers. If a pegboard is securely installed, it is strong enough to take some shelving, too. An arrangement of well-designed pots and utensils, with a shelf of cookbooks above it, can be an inexpensive and handsome addition to most kitchens.

The counters in many large kitchens are poorly planned in relation to the sink or stove. Other kitchens are so small that they have insufficient counter and work space. A possible solution, easily made or contracted out for a reasonable price, is shown on page 90. It consists of a movable cabinet/counter on casters, preferably topped with butcher block. Butcher block is one of the finest surfaces for kitchen work, and is, by the way, a good material to consider for new counters. Unfortunately, it is expensive. The cabinet/counter in the sketch has sliding doors on one side and provides a fairly large and convenient additional storage area for pots. It can even be rolled to the dining table.

If your kitchen has insufficient cabinet space, it would be expensive to add new ones and difficult to match the existing ones. An open shelving arrangement such as the one shown in the sketch on page 90 could be added in any size. This kind of shelf looks best when made of fairly heavy stock lumber such as 1 1/4 or 1 1/2 inch. It can be made with a back that is fastened to the wall or it can be open and fastened with heavy angle irons. If installed at eye level, two shelf surfaces are at a serviceable height, and hooks below the bottom shelf will hold cups or hanging tools.

In many small kitchens, especially in apartment houses, there isn't enough space for even a small table. But sometimes there is enough room in front of a window to install a smaller counter. A heavy, Formica-covered shelf, fastened with wooden cleats or angle irons, can provide an adequate breakfast or snack surface, as long as the minimum depth is 12 inches.

19/ Classic Makeshifts

Need and ingenuity have always given rise to creative problem solving. In furnishings, the solutions that have stood the test of time could be called *classic makeshifts*.

In the preceding sections I have already dealt with many classic makeshifts. Here I explain these effective design solutions in somewhat greater detail. The specific examples given require only simple tools and skills.

One of the best materials for a number of projects is the flush door. These doors are available in lumber yards in widths of 24 to 32 inches, normally 76 inches long, for around $10. They are lightweight, consisting of wood frames with plywood glued to both sides. The least expensive doors are made of a low-grade mahogany (Lauan) veneer, smoothly sanded and ready for finishing or painting. Be sure to buy the correct size, since these hollow doors cannot be cut or trimmed more than a fraction of an inch.

If you have never used flush doors, you might worry about their strength. Actually, they are sturdy enough for any normal work or seating, and because of the hollow construction there will be little or no warpage. For a little more money, you can buy flush doors in birch plywood and other veneers; for a very substantial classic makeshift, solid-core doors are still within a reasonable price range.

I have mentioned flush doors as a good work surface for counters and built-in desks; you can easily create a freestanding desk, also, with a flush door. Two double-drawer file cabinets or one file cabinet combined with any other small cabinet of the same height are all you need. File cabinets can be bought in different colors, or old file cabinets can be spray-painted. In fact, stores selling used office furnishings often have very inexpensive files on sale, since many business firms are switching to the more sophisticated lateral files.

An easy way to finish the work surface/door is to coat it with boiled linseed oil. One or two applications—rubbing in the oil in the direction of the wood grain and sanding or steel-wooling lightly between coats—followed by an occasional coat of wax from time to time, will form a protective and acceptable wood finish. Painting requires more time and effort. Covering flush doors with plastic laminates or linoleum is another possibility.

Flush doors also make good tables. A dining table can be created using either the legs available in hardware stores (metal legs must be fastened close to the corners in order to catch the inner wood frames of the door) or sawhorse bases. Even cheaper are the special brackets sold to make sawhorses from mail-order firms or hardware stores. Good quality lumber, too, will give you clean and sturdy leg supports. The edges of 2 x 4s have to be sanded and can be painted or left raw.

Plywood dining table on sawhorses.

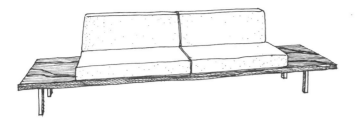

A simple, inexpensive sofa made of a flush door and foam pillows.

Another excellent use of flush doors is for sofas, or for a combination sofa and end table. I mentioned this possibility when I discussed living areas (see also p. 104) but the sketch shown here explains more clearly how to construct it. A 3- or 4-inch-thick foam mattress sitting on a flush door raised on legs makes a comfortable sofa. The sofa can extend right across a room, and the ends of the doors provide a table surface area for lamps, books, etc.

Wall-hung shelving, using standards and brackets, has been mentioned as a simple and cheap method. An even quicker way of creating shelves is with boards supported on bricks or concrete blocks. The bricks or blocks are available in lumber yards or building supply enterprises, but they often can be found abandoned or obtained from a builder or demolition contractor. Glass blocks for building are rarely used these days, but they too can be found or bought from businesses specializing in building materials. The shelves themselves can be cut from plywood or solid wood or can be purchased in stores or lumber yards carrying assortments of readymade shelves. Note that shelving made with bricks or blocks is unsteady when more than three or four levels are used.

The quickest and cheapest way to create low bookshelves: bricks and boards.

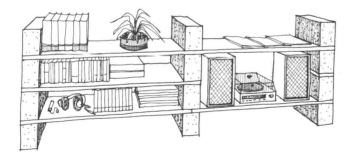

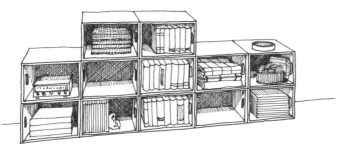

Shelving using milk crates.

Another inexpensive storage or shelving system consists of crates or boxes. The proverbial "orange crate" or packing crate is not very suitable since the wood is unfinished and full of splinters. Milk crates can be bought from suppliers or sometimes from supermarkets. Most suppliers have switched to metal crates, which may be hard to find on sale, but the few wooden milk crates still around make excellent storage units. Milk crates and some types of packing crates are quite well made, square and sanded; they can be used the way they are or painted.

A makeshift table can be made out of large wooden spools for telephone and other cables. These spools come in different sizes—the smaller ones perfectly scaled for coffee tables or end tables, and the larger ones just right for dining tables. If the wooden slats are loose or uneven they may have to be renailed. I know of no special source for new cable spools. One can frequently obtain the empty spools just by asking the telephone company.

Tables made from cable spools.

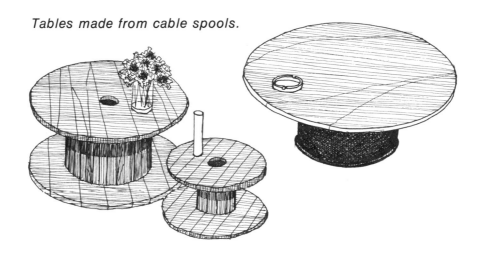

Platform beds can be quite easily built without workshop facilities. The platform can be made of sheets of plywood or chipboard, or with flush doors. If you use flush doors, you will need more than one to get the desired width and also some kind of frame to hold the doors together. Platform beds look best and work best when raised on a base to a height of 14 to 16 inches including the mattress. The base can be constructed to hold two doors together, or to reinforce the sheets of plywood. Some kind of trim around the edges gives a more finished look; whether it is in a natural finish or painted is a matter of choice.

Classic makeshifts are often found objects, or objects that were made for other purposes. The list of possibilities could be endless. Consider the cut-off pieces of heavy timber discarded on construction sites. Timber 12 by 12 inches, or even heavier stock, when cut off neatly (square) with a power saw, can make excellent small tables or coffee tables. It is a time-honored tradition in small towns to set aside a certain area in town dumps for objects that might be of use to others. Some towns even arrange these areas as trading spots, and citizens, poor and rich alike, try to find useful things thrown out by their neighbors. In large cities, people who live in the more expensive neighborhoods can sometimes be seen carefully sifting through piles of furnishings and objects put on sidewalks for pickup by the sanitation department. Of course you should not use real junk simply because it might be free. But it is a challenge to find beauty in unexpected places and to develop the courage to use and live with found objects. For years I have admired the beautiful patterns and textures on manhole covers and even taken "rubbings" of these patterns. I have never come across a manhole cover abandoned or for sale, but one could be marvelous as a table base or purely as decoration.

20/Antiques/ Recycled Furniture

United States customs law defines "antiques" as works of art, pieces of furniture, or decorative objects created or produced over 100 years ago; for certain objects the legal date for antique status is before 1830. Most genuine antiques of that vintage or older are way out of the average budget range. The most popular and influential periods for interior decorators are the eighteenth-century French and English styles. But now it is difficult even for affluent clients to buy real eighteenth-century pieces. The best of these furnishings are in museums or private collections; many of the furnishings sold in antique stores are of questionable ancestry.

However, remember that the label "antique" does not always mean "well-designed." The eighteenth century saw as many examples of bad design as our present era, and certainly the nineteenth century produced some real horrors. It is important to evaluate antiques as carefully as anything made today. I would even say that no one "period" in design is better than another. There is only good design and bad design.

Popularity in furniture styles fluctuates the way fashions do. Victorian furnishings were considered funny or bad until about 1950. At that time contemporary designers began to realize that there was indeed a good deal of merit in many of the designs from the last century, and what had been banished to attics or junk stores became fashionable once again. More recently Art Deco, the prevalent style of the 1930s, has been rediscovered, and after several well-publicized exhibitions and magazine articles, furnishings from that period are rapidly becoming collectors' items. The intrinsic quality of old or new furniture has to do with design, materials, proportion, craftsmanship, and decorative detail—not with fashion. But since I have earlier explained why reproductions are generally unacceptable as well-designed objects, I must repeat here that many old furnishings were also copies and reproductions of former eras. Some collectors believe that old pieces have the saving grace of age or charm or sentimentality to compensate for lack of design. I believe, however, that there are enough pieces with good design qualities in any period. This is certainly true for American furniture of the last century and the eighteenth century, and in any case your best chances for finding reasonable buys are in American, rather than in European, furniture.

Famous auction galleries and elegant antique stores are obviously not for the budget-minded; but it is a good idea to become acquainted with the best pieces available, perhaps by looking at the finest examples in a museum. For really good buys the best sources are country auctions, country antique dealers, and those dealers who carry a combination of used furniture and antiques. If you become really interested and have the time and patience, estate auctions can also be good sources. Lastly, there are many permanent and temporary "flea markets," and in rural regions "tag" sales or garage sales are frequent happenings.

If you have never been to a country auction or its equivalent in a city (auctions of reasonably priced furnishings), you are in for a treat. Even if you do not bid on anything, the whole atmosphere of these auctions is fun; indeed, many people enjoy auctions as much as theatrical performances. You must have a fair idea of what you are looking for (take along your plans) so you won't buy a "bargain" for which you have no use. And before you bid, you should have some idea of the quality, design, and price of furnishings that interest you.

Late eighteenth-century and early nineteenth-century chests of drawers are often excellent buys. The simple oak furniture made in many parts of the country during the last century is still quite readily available. A well-designed

Several examples of inexpensive "antiques."

pine or oak chest might come up for auction or might be on sale in a country antique store for around $20. You will not get a museum piece for that price, and the chances are that it will require stripping, refinishing, and possibly some regluing. But these simple American chests look particularly good with contemporary furniture, have lasting interest, and are good investments and real bargains to boot. Old chairs, too, can be real "finds." There are solid oak chairs, rocking chairs, caned chairs, carved chairs, and real Victorian chairs with lots of decorative details. A set of four simple, handsome oak dining chairs will probably be cheaper than four new chairs. The combination of a modern table with four old chairs can work well: the chairs might need only simple refinishing. Many antique dealers strip old furniture and refinish it before selling it, and the extra charge for that service is fairly reasonable. Bentwood chairs have become so fashionable that the really old ones are hard to get and are expensive, whereas the new ones, made by the same processes and the same manufacturers, are cheaper.

The best way to develop an understanding of the qualities of antiques is to go "antiquing" from time to time and to attend several auctions. You will soon be able to develop at least a fair understanding of values and prices and to spot a good piece even in a junk store or flea market. If you become seriously interested in the subject, books and magazines are plentiful. The kinds of antiques that I recommend are mainly American "country furniture," which is quite different from the more elegant formal furniture made for wealthy city residents of the same period (the eighteenth and nineteenth centuries). But basic design qualities do not depend upon the date. If you like something made in the early part of this century or even as recently as twenty or thirty years ago, it seems to me that your judgment, based on design criteria and personal preference, is more valid than labels attached to objects by the United States Customs Service or by decorative art historians.

When buying antiques or used furniture, concentrate on chests, cabinets, tables, and chairs, rather than sofas and other upholstered pieces. Wooden furniture is either in good condition or will require refinishing—a process that is not terribly expensive. Any old upholstered piece will probably need new fabric and reupholstery. Bedding laws require that upholsterers strip furniture completely and fumigate it, so by the time you have paid for complete reupholstery and new fabric, the bargain has usually become a folly. Also, modern furniture is more comfortable than some of the rather stiff and formal upholstered period pieces. The exceptions are some old rocking chairs and chairs made with slipseat upholstery (seats and backs which can be removed from the frame for reupholstering). A famous nineteenth-century design, considered one of the forerunners of contemporary design, is the adjustable lounge chair designed by William Morris. Many "Morris" chairs have been made since, and they do appear for sale at fair prices. Although rather bulky, they can be interesting and comfortable accent pieces in a contemporary setting.

Blanket chests, from heavily carved to simple pine, used to be standard pieces of furniture in American households. Handsome chests can be found quite easily and are useful for storage, seating, and extra table surface. Some old steamer trunks or seamen's chests, too, are available for those with small budgets. The list of old objects for good prices is endless: from plant stands to tables to hutches, the antique markets have some fine examples. When certain pieces become fashionable, they also become rare and expensive. In 1960 it was possible to find a handsome old rolltop desk for below $100. Today those desks in good condition fetch prices near $500—obviously no longer good buys. Round oak extension tables were quite cheap until 1965. Because many designers and design-conscious people saw their value (strong, practical, and good-looking) their prices have also climbed, and it is doubtful whether good buys can be found today.

The specific examples that I have mentioned are all American pieces. This is because it is simply much harder to find good antiques from other countries for low prices. Rarely is an Oriental or European piece sold in the bargain price range. But should you find any affordable furniture or decorative arts from other countries, these, too, can be mixed most successfully with modern furnishings and combined with some American antiques.

In the previous chapter I pointed out that one can find perfectly fine things in unexpected places such as town dumps. Therefore, I certainly would not discourage anybody on a tight budget from looking for good buys in used furniture stores. I stress again that the borderline between antiques and used furnishings is not clearly defined. If you have trained your eye and consciously developed some understanding of design criteria and perhaps of historic furniture, dealers of used furniture could become excellent resources for you. Many rather well-to-do design professionals refer to some of their best pieces as "early Salvation Army." To reject anything used out of false pride does not make sense if one realizes that priceless antiques are actually used furniture. So by all means check out the Salvation Army or Goodwill stores if you want to.

And if you become interested in antiques, the payoff might come not only in finding bargains, but also in the joy of discovery and the pleasure of becoming a collector.

21/Lamps/ Lighting

There are three important aspects to lighting: function, aesthetics, and health. The last factor is often ignored, with fatigue and physical discomfort the result. Poor lighting can harm your eyes and adversely affect your mood and behavior. While in most cases poor lighting means insufficient illumination, for certain activities you will not always need large quantities of lighting. High-intensity fluorescent lights for a conversation group in a living room, or several bright lamps in a dining space, create an obviously inappropriate mood. Lighting can create atmosphere and is a significant consideration for interior design.

For normal residential lighting, a few basic facts should help you, even in the selection of simple portable lamps. Most frequently, incandescent lamps are the kind used in homes. While they are not terribly efficient in terms of energy consumption (more energy is converted into heat than light), they are the most satisfactory sources of home lighting. The other type is fluorescent lighting. It is far more efficient, but because of its uneven spectrum, colors tend to be distorted. Fluorescent lighting is appropriate for many tasks—in kitchens, at desks, in any special work areas—and "warm" fluorescent lamps are now available which give off a more natural light than the "cool" bluish type. Often, the best lighting effect in terms of color can be achieved by having a mixture of incandescent and fluorescent types in the same place, and this is usually easier on the eyes as well.

The technical measurement of lighting is expressed in *lumens* (not in watts) and light cast on surfaces is expressed in *footcandles*. Lighting designers have arrived at specific recommendations for a variety of tasks: for reading, a level of 60 footcandles; for sewing on dark materials, 150 footcandles; and for walking in a corridor, 20 footcandles. It is unlikely that you will purchase lamps for home use with any of these figures in mind, and indeed there is no need to do so. It helps, however, to know what job each lamp is supposed to do and be aware of the existence of all this information, should you have some really difficult problem to solve. The personnel in better lighting supply houses are often knowledgeable enough to give you very accurate advice.

Lighting can be used in direct or indirect form. An example of direct lighting is a reading or desk lamp, which has a reflector directing the light onto a particular surface. Indirect lighting might be built-in cove lighting, or a ceiling pendant (hanging light) which throws light against a white ceiling and illuminates the space through the reflected light from the ceiling or wall surfaces. Frequently, the most disturbing feature of home lighting is the glare. If an exposed lamp (lighting specialists call a bulb a *lamp*) hangs from the ceiling close to eye level, the glare is very disturbing. And many portable lamps emit too much glare. Sometimes this is because too strong a lamp has been used. For instance, shades or globes made of translucent glass or plastic are very popular, often well designed, and inexpensive. But with such lamps you should be very careful to limit the intensity of the light source. Since glare is unpleasant as well as unhealthy, remember that a general background level of light, with higher intensity for certain tasks, is always desirable. In other words, if you have a strong desk or reading lamp, it is probably better to have some additional general illumination in the same room, lest you experience constant glare due to the difference between the illumination on the task and the surrounding dark area.

A fairly simple rule for good lighting is based on distribution. One single light source in a given space may give off enough illumination and provide enough footcandles of light for specific purposes. But a single concentrated source of light is far less pleasant than a series of smaller light sources distributed throughout a room. Perhaps the best-designed lighting systems are those that are hardly visible. Unfortunately, these schemes usually can be accomplished only during building or remodeling. Examples are cove lighting, valance lighting, lighting installed above hung ceilings, and recessed lighting into ceilings. But even with a built-in lighting design, it is always nice to have a small "pool" or accent of light somewhere else in the room. Often these small accents contribute little or nothing to the actual level of lighting, but they do provide a visual excitement and sparkle. In our age of energy problems it may be wrong to suggest any nonessential consumption of energy, but the accents or pools of light can be created with very low-level wattage.

Most lighting for homes will consist of portable lamps, ceiling-mounted fixtures, or wall-mounted fixtures; all three types fall under the heading of portable lighting. Table lamps and floor lamps are available in a good choice of high-quality contemporary design. Manufacturers of traditional lamps tend to mix up decorative accessories and sculpture with lighting. The result is often ungainly. Of course, not all contemporary lamps are great design either. One way to evaluate the quality of design is by analyzing what the lamp is supposed to do, whether the materials are appropriate and well made, and whether the overall design is well proportioned and functional. After all, lamps are tools in a way, designed to give light.

The floor lamps and table lamps shown in the sketch on page 174 are classics and are available in many price ranges. The shaded sources of light eliminate glare, the height of the shade shedding light on a table or book assures a degree of control, and the shade assures a soft general illumination in addition to giving task-oriented light. Whether the bases are metal or wood, marble or ceramic, remains a matter of choice; as long as they are well-crafted simple designs, the chances are that they will meet our design criteria. Of the table, desk, and floor lamps shown, the one which is basically a drafting lamp is an excellent and flexible device. Since all parts of the lamp move, the shade can be turned toward the ceiling for reflected light, or it can be turned toward a wall, bookshelves, or paintings to highlight special areas.

Wall-mounted lamps are made as "pin-up" types to be plugged into an outlet, or as permanently installed sources if there is a wall receptacle. The appearance does not vary greatly, and a good many wall-mounted lamps are available for either type of installation. Some small pin-up lamps have carefully designed reflectors to control the amount and direction of emitted light, a factor particularly useful if you read in bed. Couples often suffer when one person wants to read while the other wishes to sleep. Perhaps the appropriate light can do a good deal toward preventing marital discord!

One very handsome wall fixture is based on an opaque glass or plexiglass cylinder. Such fixtures come with arms or rods of varying length, some with uplight and downlight, some with a single lamp. They look equally good in a formal, symmetrical arrangement (for instance, on each side of a fireplace or focal piece of furniture) and used singly (over a chair, sofa, or wherever a wall outlet or the need for a light exists). Swing-arm or scissor-arm pin-up wall lamps are particularly suitable as reading lamps in those spaces where the floor space is very limited and where a floor lamp would look cluttered. Some of these pin-up lights can be found in electrical supply stores catering to builders and architectural specifiers. The fact that many of these fixtures are designed for public spaces or even outdoor spaces does not make them any less successful for interior hallways or other rooms.

Inexpensive overhead or ceiling lamps should be selected for simplicity. Imitation chandeliers are neither good design nor cheap. Highly decorative, crystal-trimmed, or Tiffany-type fixtures are poor imitations when they are cheap. An original Tiffany lamp, for example, will probably cost well over $1,000. The more contemporary designs, simple in their conception, are really more elegant, even though they are inexpensive. One of the all-time classics is the globe-shaped pendant, which comes in many sizes, mounted directly on the ceiling surface, or dropped on stems or cords. Globe lights are very reasonably priced. Also quite suitable are a number of decorative but well-designed shade-type pendants which are Scandinavian-influenced and which can be found in a variety of materials, from painted metal to brass to plexiglass.

Many of the portable lamps described and illustrated here are easier to locate in specialized lighting stores than in department stores. Electrical supply houses, too, will be a good source.

For kitchens, bathrooms, and workrooms, fluorescent fixtures are often best and cheapest. Square (2 x 2 feet or 4 x 4 feet) and rectangular (1 x 4 feet and up) fixtures with a plastic or plexiglass cover are extremely efficient and quite good-looking. They can be purchased with two, four, or eight tubes of fluorescent lamps and thus present a wide choice of output. A good fixture of that type in a kitchen will normally be better-looking and far more appropriate than an elaborate or "cute" lamp. This is true for bathrooms, too. The popular crystal-type bathroom lamps are not only expensive but give off far too little light. If you are concerned about the color of your complexion in a bathroom, you must be sure to buy daylight or standard warm fluorescent tubes.

I mentioned recessed spotlights, or "Hi Hats," in connection with eating

Typical lighting fixtures: ceiling, floor, table, wall-hung.

spaces. These fixtures, also available very cheaply in electrical supply houses, are fairly easy to install if the ceiling is hollow. They cannot be recessed into an existing concrete ceiling, and in most high-rise buildings the plaster ceilings will not be deep enough. But they should certainly be considered as a good design solution for a variety of spaces where the ceiling can accommodate them.

A generally worthwhile addition for ceiling fixtures, and sometimes for portable lamps, too, is a dimmer switch. A dimmer costs less than $10 and can be installed easily in a standard wall switch. It gives you much flexibility in creating mood or atmosphere; the effect of dimmed lights can be very pleasant, for instance, at a dinner party.

A good way to create either soft background lighting or accent lighting is to place a lamp at ground level and let the light shine up. To avoid glare the lamp must be shielded with louvers, directed away from any sight lines, or placed behind a piece of furniture (such as the sofa). A "can" is an excellent device for creating accent lighting. Lighting stores carry them, usually equipped with concentric louvers (it works pretty much like a "Hi Hat" placed upside down); the best effect is achieved with a spot or floodlamp. These fixtures are not expensive, but if you are ambitious you can cut costs even further and make your own out of a large empty can, attaching a socket to the inside, and spraying the can white or black on the outside.

A similar uplight effect can be created with a clamp-on photographer's lamp. These clamps cost around $2 apiece and hold the type of projector or floodlamps suitable for spotlighting. They usually come equipped with a cord and switch; if they do not have a switch, a line switch can easily be installed. Photographer's lamps can be clamped to the rear leg of a sofa or large chair and directed with accuracy against the ceiling or toward a wall or painting. Such clamp-on lamps must be hidden or shielded to avoid glare. If you have some large plants or indoor trees, the lamps can be most effective directed straight up through the leaves creating highlights and shadows on the leaves. The freestanding, shielded "can" can be used for these effects, too.

A third possibility along similar lines is to use commercially available spotlights. These range from simple, inexpensive ball- or bullet-shaped adjustable devices to rather sophisticated spotlights with ground lenses for accurate control (almost like theatrical spotlights). The simple ones are quite adequate for our purposes. Finished in black or white, they are made to spotlight paintings, sculpture, or wall hangings. They can also be used to flood a curtain (or any other wall area) with light and give reflected illumination to the room.

If your hallway ceiling has an ugly glass fixture, remove the cover and insert a pivot spot attachment—the kind of lighting that is normally used in galleries. Or, removing the fixture and retaining the porcelain socket can provide a good way to use the large, filament-type clear glass globe lamps. These interesting and well-designed products act as a combination lamp and decorative fixture.

Among the finest lighting systems are track-mounted ceiling spotlights (see p. 51), similar to those used in art galleries. These light tracks must be installed by an electrician or someone who is very able with electrical installations—and that is the catch. They are not expensive, they are totally flexible (you can always buy additional plug-in spots at a later date), and since they reflect light back from wall surfaces, they can almost serve as the only illumination in a space. But unless you are ready for a fairly permanent investment in lighting and unless you have permission from your apartment manager to undertake such an installation, track lighting is best for those who own their own homes.

For valance lighting or counter lighting under cabinets you need only be able to handle a power drill. Valance lighting, as the name implies, can be installed behind a curtain valance, or it can be used on a valance running over a desk or storage or bookshelf arrangement. Its advantage is that it is an indirect lighting system of very reasonable cost, with the exception of the labor. For undercabinet kitchen or storage wall lighting, small strip lighting, ready to install, can be found in lighting supply or hardware stores. Some of these devices are incandescent showcase lamps rather than fluorescent types, and some are the "thin-line" type. A visit to an electrical supply house can reveal any number of well-designed ingenious lighting devices for less cost than the cheapest store-bought lamp.

I have already mentioned the Japanese rice paper shades in the section on eating spaces. They most often come in globe or bubble form and because of their very light weight can be installed directly on an electric cord. These lanterns come in many shapes and sizes and can be installed just about anywhere, hanging low over a table for instance, or covering the simple porcelain socket in an existing ceiling fixture.

A final word about the quality of light in general: all artificial light depends upon the reflective qualities of the surfaces which it strikes. Dark surfaces and textured surfaces absorb more light than do light-colored and smooth ones. The best fixtures will not be as efficient in rooms painted dark colors. Another factor to keep in mind is maintenance. Plastic shielding and other covers on lights must be cleaned from time to time. The life expectancy of lamps is finite, and toward the end of its life-span a lamp begins to lose efficiency. Public buildings have carefully programmed maintenance schedules for replacing lamps and cleaning fixtures. It is wise to consider all these factors for the best choice of lighting.

22/ Windows/ Window Coverings

Many people assume that curtains are the only way to deal with windows. I suggest that the first question you should ask yourself is whether you need a window covering at all, and if the answer is yes, whether curtains are the right solution. If you have a beautiful view—with privacy—or if you live in a high-rise building with a spectacular view of the city and have no neighbors to look in, or if some of your windows face into a private or semiprivate area, it may be a good solution to do nothing at all to the windows. Or, especially in older buildings, the architectural detailing of the windows is often handsome and curtains would detract from it.

Curtains do not necessarily make a room more elegant or handsome. There are, however, several good reasons for designing some kind of window treatment. The most common ones are privacy and light control. If you do not want your neighbors to look into your home, if you need to keep strong sunlight out, or if you want to be able to darken a bedroom in order to sleep late—all these are good reasons for window coverings. Poorly placed windows, unevenly placed windows, or messy-looking windows, encumbered with poorly finished radiators and uninteresting woodwork, might benefit from window coverings, too. In those cases the negative architectural features can sometimes be helped by a screenlike window treatment, whether with curtains, screens, or shades. Another reason for window treatments, especially curtains, is that windows can look like black holes at night, unless there is a view such as city lights or a lighted garden.

Traditional curtains with overdrapes, side panels, valances, and trimmings are neither good design nor fashionable. These elaborate treatments were popular during the Victorian era and in the early part of this century. Today, light and air and a relationship to the outdoors are considered better design. Above all, light window treatments are far cheaper than elaborate, stagelike curtains and draperies.

The least expensive and most elementary window coverings are shades. The best-designed shades are the simple ones, in white or light-colored materials, with a simple straight edge and a functional pullstring. If your building does not provide such shades, they can be purchased in varying qualities and price ranges. The very cheap plastic ones tear easily; perhaps a slightly more expensive fabric content shade is worthwhile. Even white shades can be made lightproof—a somewhat more expensive material treatment. If you live in a building of some architectural interest, whether apartment house or private residence, it is also well to remember that white or light-colored shades might look better from the outside. For some rooms, such as children's rooms, bathrooms, or playrooms, a decorated shade is fun. Window shades can be laminated with fabrics and some wallpapers.

The matchstick bamboo shades are also well designed and inexpensive; these are available in most Oriental import stores, in small boutiques, and in some department stores. Matchstick shades can be found in the appropriate size for most windows. They should be bought somewhat larger than the width of the window (it would be a rare coincidence to find them a perfect fit) and then cut to the proper width with heavy shears or strong scissors, using a small saw for the end pieces. They are hung on two small cuphooks, which usually come with the shades. Matchstick shades allow enough privacy during daylight hours and provide a pleasant warm atmosphere at night. They do not give nighttime privacy, however, and for bedrooms you may need ordinary shades in addition to or instead of matchstick shades. Most of these matchstick shades are sold in natural colors (bamboo) and some are available in white; either is most attractive. Needless to say, this kind of window covering precludes the need for curtains.

Many apartment buildings provide Venetian blinds as standard equipment. A perfectly acceptable window treatment, blinds offer flexibility for sunlight control as well as total privacy. In recent years a new type of narrow slat blind has been developed which is extremely handsome as a textured window covering. It offers the same flexibility as the old-fashioned Venetian blinds, but is better designed in its detail and working mechanism and much better-looking. Unfortunately, these blinds are not cheap. However, they are still a good buy if they are used as the only window treatment. They come in colors and metallic finishes, but most often in white. "Levolor" is one well-known brand.

"Levolor" blinds.

Another possibility might be any of the vertical blinds sold in specialty stores. These range somewhat higher in price than ordinary Venetian blinds, but again they present the advantages of a more finished appearance and more flexibility in light control. Many of the vertical blinds can be pivoted in any direction, can be closed completely for privacy, and can be pulled open like curtains. The best designs in that category are the fabric or plastic vertical blinds that are wider than the normal Venetian blinds. Actually, these elegant blinds are marketed for commercial rather than residential use, but they might be a worthwhile consideration as a single window covering rather than the combination of shades and curtains.

Stores dealing in shades and blinds often carry wooden slats or bamboo blinds and shades. The wooden slats are wider than the matchstick kind and

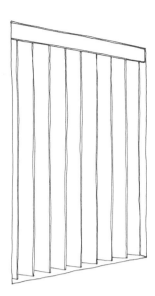

Vertical blinds.

somewhat more expensive. Those made in an overlapping construction provide ample privacy. A good many commercial products, inspired by well-designed handcrafted and handwoven blinds, combine wooden slats and interwoven strands of fabric. Unfortunately, the commercially made products do not have the charm and character of the originals. They are also a good deal costlier than the simple wooden slat or bamboo blinds.

Wooden shutters can still be found in many old homes. If you live in an old townhouse with shuttered windows, why not try to restore the shutters if they are in salvageable condition? The windows in old houses are often much more elaborately designed than in new buildings. The walls are heavier, and the windows often sit in a deep reveal, if not a bay. That kind of window should not be covered over with curtains. Sometimes the woodwork around the sides

Matchstick shades.

of windows is nicely paneled, and it makes sense to expose the original wood if possible. Also, a deep window can be used for a window seat—a good feature to add if none exists. Shutters in general are not expensive but do require a good deal of work for installation. While it might be excessive to cover large windows with shutters, they are a fine choice for smaller ones, for bedroom windows, or for bathroom windows. In fact, shutters work very well in bathrooms because they provide privacy and ventilation and do not require much maintenance.

Wooden shutters.

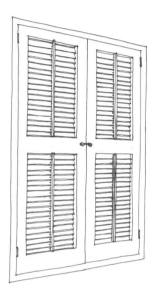

Along the lines of more time-consuming do-it-yourself projects are window screens. Most popular are the reasonably priced Japanese Shoji screens, available in special window-covering shops. The custom-made version of these screens is fairly expensive to buy and have installed. However, if you are handy, you might try making simple wooden frames as sliding screens; there are many options for filler material. While the traditional Japanese screens have insets made of rice paper or parchment (the more expensive ones have plastic), a homemade or custom-made screen installation can have fabric, caning, paper, or plastic. Lightweight screens can be hung from double or triple ceiling tracks, but even then they will take up a certain amount of wall or window space when pushed open. They are a rather complex window treatment and should probably only be considered if you are handy and if you have to contend with a difficult or ugly window placement.

Sliding screens for windows.

I have mentioned that heavy, elaborate, and expensive curtains are not necessary for well-designed interiors. In fact, the best and most reasonably priced fabric in most cases is a lightweight one known as *casement fabric*. The simplest kind of casement fabric is fishnet, but there is a vast array of interesting patterns in fairly open, very open, or fairly tight weaves, including a range of fibers from fine to coarse. One of the cheapest fabrics is lightweight linen, but with the many man-made fibers on the market, one cannot really say that one fiber is preferable to another. For windows that need only some softening and some warmth at night, an open weave will be best. Open-weave curtains can remain drawn and still allow brightness and some degree of view of the outdoors. Yet such fabrics provide privacy during daytime and even screen out any architectural defects around the window area.

Of course an open casement is not the answer to every problem. Sometimes a heavier fabric, a printed fabric, or a richly colored fabric may be desired, and at times a heavier fabric will eliminate the need for shades or blinds. If you do use a very light fabric in a bedroom or other area where privacy is important, you obviously have to use shades or blinds in addition. If a room needs protection from sunlight it may also be important to use a somewhat heavier material.

Casement-type curtains are not lined—another money-saving feature. The lining of curtains has its origin in the need to protect costly fabrics, such as silk, and to give a fuller body to the folds formed by the curtain arrangement. Unless a space has to be absolutely dark during daytime or the lining is used to control heat and energy, I feel that lined curtains should be avoided.

When you do use curtains, you must decide whether to cover individual windows only, or whether to go wall-to-wall and floor-to-ceiling. Individual curtains can be quite beautiful and there is a good deal of choice for the kind of treatment that might be considered.

The simple traverse rod or brass rod curtains are best for most uses. Since they require only one set of curtain hardware, they are also the cheapest. Café curtains, or half or three-quarter curtains, are also reasonably priced and can be bought readymade in almost any size. I believe that straightforward café curtains are better than ruffled and trimmed ones, and I know they are cheaper. In fact, a visit to the curtain department of a large store will reveal any number of treatments. Valances, lambrequins, cornices, and many other authentic or imitative styles of window coverings are marketed.

Covering a whole wall with a curtain is often a good idea, even if from a pure design point of view it might represent a bit of theatrical fakery. A window wall covered floor-to-ceiling and wall-to-wall with a fabric can provide a soft, luxurious, and unifying design element in a room and at the same time eliminate from view such eyesores as columns, pipes, and radiators. Many stores sell readymade curtains in panels or pairs, and if the length does not fit exactly, it is fairly easy to shorten them. For the width, it is simply a matter of figuring out how many widths or panels are required. If you install wall-to-wall curtains on a single traverse ceiling rod (which is best), you might want to put several individual panels together in order to arrive at two large pairs. Normally, one figures 100 percent fullness for pleated curtains, which means that a width of 10 feet, for example, needs 20 feet of fabric to result in soft folds. If you make your own curtains, you must figure on that fullness, plus the proper length for each panel, including hems at the bottom and pleats at the top. When you buy readymade curtains, the extra fullness is already there, and you simply measure the width (or read it on the label) for the finished panel or pair.

A good many special devices for making curtain pleats can be found in stores. The conventional French pleats or pinch pleats are rather difficult to sew. Tapes, curtain pins, and hardware can be used to make pleats without special sewing skills. With one of these gadgets any wide fabric, such as sheets, can be used as curtain material.

Here are a few helpful hints for some special ways of covering windows, especially for those who want to try something unexpected.

I have described casement fabric as being something like fish netting. Why not tack a *real* lightweight net, sold in stores dealing with theater supplies, onto a simple wooden rod or directly to a window trim? It will not give you privacy, but it will soften the window and give it a finished, unusual look. An even more esoteric window treatment is the use of chains or beads. While buying chains or beads in large quantity is pretty expensive, you might be able to find a special source for lightweight chains or "popit" beads or bamboo beads. Window coverings of that type have been used in elegant public spaces and hotels and can be an exciting design feature.

If you are handy and if you can sew, you can also consider making your own shades. Rollers and hardware for shades can be bought separately (or existing ones can be taken off); making a shade out of fabric can be inexpensive and decorative. Of course the fabric must not be too heavy, lest it present problems when rolled up, and there should be a small wooden strip at the bottom of the shade so that it will remain straight when pulled down.

A rather delightful cafe curtain treatment for a kitchen, a bathroom, or a child's room can be achieved by buying the cheapest kind of solid linen or cotton cafe curtains. Buying two pairs in two different colors and then installing them in checkerboard fashion will give you your own "design," easily matched or compatible with whatever color scheme you might have.

My last suggestion is not a real window treatment as such, and it cannot be done with too many windows. It is the use of plants to pretty much "cover" a window (see p. 53). If the window has a sill or perhaps a shelf at sill height, a few fairly tall plants, combined with some hanging plants, can give enough cover to the glass area so that no curtain or shade is needed. Ideally it should be a window receiving enough sunlight for the plants, and it should be a window that does not require privacy. If the window is fairly tall, you might be able to mount a glass shelf (see p. 88) about halfway up the window and have another level, or even two, of standing and hanging plants. Along the same lines, it is also possible to use a window with some shelving for a collection of glasses or bottles; or you can hang some pieces of stained glass salvaged from an old building in front of the window.

In summary, it is important to get away from the conventional decorator dictum that a window must have an elaborate and formal curtain arrangement. When considering window treatments, think in personal terms.

23/ Products

We use hundreds of products every day at home and at work, and I am sure one could come up with some interesting statistics on the number of objects that the average family owns. Every single object has certain design qualities. Some things are not *designed* in the usual sense of the meaning but have a particularly high design quality based on their straightforward function and utility. Simple tools like screwdrivers and utilitarian objects like paperclips can be handsome and elegant. A paperclip, a wood screw, a piece of hardware, or a ballpoint pen can also be very cheap. The design quality of everyday objects matters greatly in the overall apperance of our homes. Since we are inundated with advertising for countless unnecessary things and face almost unlimited choices of all kinds of products, it becomes particularly important to develop design criteria and value judgments.

One simple test in evaluating the intrinsic quality of any object is to ask whether it fulfills a need or meets some purpose. Look through the pages of a typical mail-order novelty catalog and try to count the useful and sensible items you can find; the chances are that there will be none! I am talking about products and household objects, not about art objects. The purpose of art can be to delight; hence decorative objects and objets d'art do not have to have a purpose beyond the intent of their creators, whatever that might have been. But it will help to view the products that we use differently from the way we might respond to a piece of sculpture, for instance. To advocate a total separation of function and decoration would be an oversimplification, but it can be a good beginning in developing critical design standards. As a rule, the simpler objects tend to be less expensive; they also tend to be better designed.

I suspect that very few people have given much thought to the design quality of matchbooks. The inexpensive matchbook is a truly good design solution. It is the added decoration—in this case, printed advertising—that takes away from the basic design quality. Much of the advertising uses very poor graphics and is ugly. At times you might find matchbooks in plain white, black, or colored covers; compare those with the typical gaudy variety from your local tobacconist or supermarket. I realize that matchbooks are not significant objects in our homes, but I purposely use this example to show how good design or bad design affects just about everything we use in our lives.

Matchbooks: good and bad.

Glassware is another example. Many water and wine glasses are quite expensive. Crystal or cut glass is a highly developed craft, and some pieces are indeed very beautiful and worth their high cost. But there is no need to spend a great deal of money on glasses if you are budget-conscious. Almost every hardware store sells simple glasses which are well proportioned, elegant, certainly functional, and far superior in design to the many oddly shaped or overdecorated glasses that cost three or four times as much. Inexpensive and

Glasses: good and bad.

well-designed glass can be found in specialty stores, department stores, and home furnishing stores. The price increases if the quality of glass is finer and thinner and if the glass is free of imperfections. However, the kind of glass shown in the sketch is a basic shape with a timeless quality. Sometimes cheaper products are better designed.

Another product which just about everybody buys at some time is a portable radio. One way of trying to evaluate the design of a radio is to ask what the important features should be? Is it sound? Is it size? Is it ease of operation or appearance? One should expect a radio to have all of these qualities as well as clearly understandable controls, dials, knobs, and, in general, an appearance expressive of its purpose. As it happens, radios and other audio products have become rather handsome in recent years; most of the more sophisticated stereo equipment is well enough designed to leave it sitting on shelves or tables, adding visual pleasure to the enjoyment of sound. But many radios have plastic cases made to look like wood, or made in the shape of model automobiles and other absurd forms. There is no doubt that a radio which is "honestly" a radio is of better design than one pretending to be something it is not.

Well-designed radio.

Consumer products often suffer from "overdesign" as manufacturers try to come up with a new, better, and above all more salable item. Although it is true that there is no ultimate design, there are certain basic shapes and objects that can hardly be improved upon. An example of an almost ultimate design is a spoon. This is based on simple facts of human anatomy; the way we take small portions of liquid can hardly be altered. If you see a spoon that has a tortured shape—one that obviously will make it difficult to eat with—it is poor design, no matter how expensive. Heavily ornamented spoons might be interesting or beautiful, but they do not measurably enhance the basic design quality. Selecting a spoon, therefore, might lead you to a simple classic shape, in a practical material such as stainless steel (no need to polish), with no ornamentation or little decoration (easier cleaning); if you follow these criteria, you will wind up with a well-designed spoon which is also quite inexpensive.

From these few examples certain basic criteria could be put into a list of key points:

- Does the object fill a need?
- Does it work?
- Have human factors been considered? (Is the handle comfortable? Can one eat with it?)
- Does it express its purpose?
- Is it made of the right material?
- Has the material been finished properly (smoothed, polished, etc.)?
- Is the quality of the material good?
- Does it have good proportions and form?
- Is it beautiful?

Notice that the question of aesthetic success comes last. If all the other questions can be answered affirmatively, the chances are that the object is also beautiful. If all these criteria have been met, the object is probably reasonably priced, too.

Well-designed clocks.

Most people are interested in the design qualities of cutlery, china, and glassware, and the sketches show some typical examples of high quality and low cost. Fortunately, there is a vast selection of these products readily available in a variety of stores. Good design and low cost can and should be kept in mind for all products that you purchase, including some more mundane objects of daily use.

Kitchen utensils can be beautiful or ugly. Plastic containers, for instance,

Examples of well-designed cutlery, china, glassware, kitchen tools, and utensils.

are at their best if they are simple and functional. The type that is available in the five-and-ten stores is often superior, and certainly much cheaper, than the fancy ones sold as gifts. Kitchen tools, pots and pans, cutting boards, bowls, and small appliances all deserve careful selection. At their best, some of these products are much more attractive than decorative objects. At their worst, they will be plain and inoffensive but at least they will not be ugly. Other household items—ashtrays, coat hangers, clocks, and wastebaskets—can be good design and good buys at the same time.

Most towns have specialty shops for "good design" merchandise, for china and glassware, or sometimes for a combination of these things with home furnishings. The larger cities all have special discount stores for glassware, pottery, and related objects, and both types of stores are excellent sources. Some stores feature kitchen utensils exclusively and are a good source for tools and functional kitchen objects. The kind of store that specializes in gifts and souvenirs is probably the most difficult one to use as a source for well-designed and reasonably priced things. I have mentioned hardware stores and five-and-ten stores. Shopping can become an adventure if you are determined to discover the best and the cheapest—sometimes in offbeat and unexpected places.

ACCESSORIES

I would say that most objects made and sold as "accessories" should be avoided. This will not only save money but will also prevent you from purchasing things of highly questionable taste. Clearly a home with no personal or decorative objects would be a rather dull place, but the kinds of things that can beautify a space or add interest and sparkle can be handsome objects *not* specifically made as centerpieces, wall plaques, or "knick-knacks." Ashtrays are an example of design to be selected for function—for form as well as appearance—and an ashtray can certainly be called an "accessory." Products needed for a great many purposes, from radios to candlesticks to vases to candy dishes, can do much to enhance the total design of a room. I am counseling against the mass-produced, cheap, or vulgar things that are marketed to make you spend money.

In addition to the things that you may need or want, there are probably

*Folk art and baskets:
beautiful and fun
to collect.*

many places in your home where some decorative or personal objects would look well. Almost anything that interests you can be used for such purposes. The types of objects that could be fun can often be quite inexpensive. For instance, simple folk art is meaningful and beautiful, and you could easily start a collection of certain types without spending much money. Colorful Mexican and South American folk art objects are available in all price ranges. Some collectibles are made out of *papier-mâché,* clay, ceramics, glass, and wood. Depending on what strikes your fancy, you might begin to collect a particular type of object, for instance, masks, simple candlesticks, or traditional figures depicting religious or mythological events or people. These objects come from many cultures, including African countries, India, and the Orient.

An even cheaper collection of decorative accessories might be seashells, rocks, minerals, or stones. A perceptive eye can sometimes spot a beautiful object in nature for the price of picking it up. If you shop in stores carrying well-designed products, you might find some beautiful plastic objects which can also be used decoratively. For instance, simple plastic boxes, widely available in most stores, can be quite elegant if grouped together, perhaps filled with beads or marbles for color as well as a personal touch.

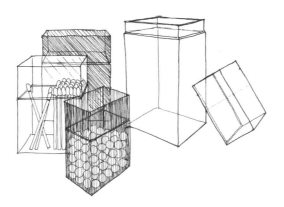

*Plastic boxes: attractive and handy
for storage and display.*

A good source for glassware might be a store selling chemical supplies, flasks, and bottles. Often the purely functional shapes of this type of fine, thin glass make handsome vases, decanters, or dishes, more beautiful than glassware made expressly for the home. One of the examples shown in the sketch on page 190 is a coffeemaker inspired by chemical glass. It makes excellent coffee using paper filters and is an ingenious and relatively inexpensive product.

Of course, glass in general is decorative. Many people enjoy collections of glass, from old bottles (quite reasonably priced in antique shops or flea markets) to modern glass or hand-blown glasswares. In recent years many craftsmen have opened small shops, usually in rural areas, which feature glassware and ceramics. The simpler ceramic dishes, bowls, mugs, and vases are not expensive and, if handmade, represent a high level of personal expression.

Personal travel mementos, family heirlooms, or just about anything that expresses a particular interest can be displayed successfully, but accessories are not necessarily an essential part of good interior design. Sometimes a few drawings or graphics or a number of plants are more interesting than the conscious addition of decorative objects.

Changing things from time to time also adds interest and variety. For example, a handsome basket can be filled with pine cones during the fall and with fresh fruit or seashells at other times.

Perhaps some of the objects that you acquire will not be considered perfect design by the experts. But a home expressing the conscious choices that you have made will be far more meaningful and certainly far cheaper than one filled with products manufactured for the express purpose of "decoration."

24/ Displaying Art

I am referring here to the traditional forms of art: painting, prints, sculpture, drawings, and photographs. But since original art is usually very expensive, I include crafts, objects, and unconventional decorative arts as suitable alternatives for display in homes.

It is important to realize that a good interior need not have art, or anything else, on every wall or on any wall. Sometimes a blank wall is far better than a "decorated" one, and a really well-designed and interesting space may at times need no works of art at all. No art is better than poor art.

In an age when the costs of original art are spiraling, it is difficult to suggest ways of acquiring good art for little money. Major artists and major art galleries are far too expensive, although they do provide the means to develop an understanding of art. Be sure to look at the best before you buy. Even if you have set yourself a small budget, it would be a mistake to walk into a store or neighborhood gallery and pick up an original or a reproduction simply because it is within your price range.

There are many young artists whose prices are reasonable. Most art schools have exhibitions of student work from time to time. Many communities have outdoor art shows or benefits where excellent artwork can be found for little money. In benefit shows, serious and well-known artists frequently donate their works, and the prices are much lower than in commercial galleries. Look for the "juried" shows rather than those where anybody can display his wares. A juried or invitational show will give you the benefit of preliminary screening by people with some background in art.

Prints, etchings, lithographs, serigraphs, or good graphics can be just as satisfying as "original" pieces. Collectors value signed prints more highly than unsigned ones, but it seems to me that the artist's signature on a print does not measurably enhance the quality of a good work. Prints, etchings, and graphics are always made in limited numbers. While the early prints reproduced from a plate or stone are more accurate and perfect than later ones, it takes a real expert to tell the difference. Serious artists do not permit more than 100 or 200 prints to be run from their original plates, and that finite number determines the considerably higher value of such prints compared to commercial reproductions—which can be printed in unlimited numbers.

Contemporary artwork is more readily available, and far cheaper, than older pieces of high quality. Not everything that is old is good; in fact, looking at old paintings in antique shops should make it clear that one must be extremely careful! With some developed knowledge and discrimination, it may be possible, however, to find some interesting old paintings, prints, or sculpture; and you might be fortunate enough to discover something of real historic or artistic value for practically no money at all.

Art does not have to "match" interiors. Nor is there any need to have modern art in contemporary interiors: very modern artwork can look splendid alongside antique furniture. The colors in paintings or watercolors do not have to match the colors in a room. Standard thematic subjects can be a real bore. The idea of using nothing but subjects related to food in a dining room makes no more sense than prescribing landscapes for living rooms and nocturnal scenes for bedrooms.

DISPLAY

Arranging a variety of pictures and "things" on a wall can be quite an art in itself. There is no set rule on whether to center a painting on a wall or above a sofa; rather, it is a matter of composition that should be decided in relation to the general balance and proportion of the room and the wall.

If you have four or more prints, drawings, or photographs, it usually works

Different ways of displaying art.

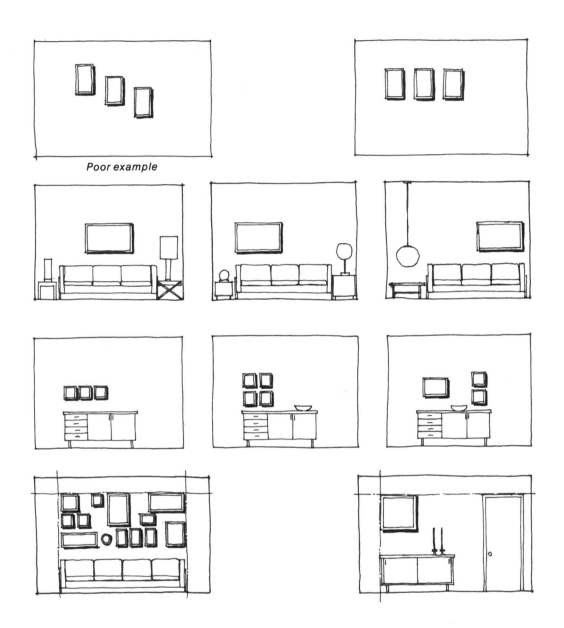

Poor example

best to arrange them in a block or in a straight line. Only a number of different-sized pictures would make a "composition" worthwhile. Unless you have a lot of experience doing this, the best guideline is to arrange the pictures within an imaginary rectangle and thus create a block composition. It is also a good idea to relate your composition or your blocks or lines of pictures to the architectural elements of the space you are using. If the top line of a grouping is almost level with the top of a door, window, or nearby bookshelves, it might as well be "lined up." This holds true for furniture. Do not hang pictures until the major pieces of furniture have been placed. A large painting or group of paintings over a sofa or big cabinet may be centered, placed off-center, or placed off-center so that the picture or composition lines up with the end of the piece of furniture.

If there is one general guide to the proper height for paintings, it is that the approximate center of the picture should be at eye level (standing). Obviously this does not hold for a very large piece of artwork, or if the artwork relates as part of a composition to another object. In other words, sometimes a print or picture hung quite low over an end table or sofa may be more interesting than at eye level. An abstract and very colorful painting or graphic piece does not have to be studied in detail and can more readily be used as an element of composition. A very delicate drawing or a map should be placed so that the details can be examined.

FRAMES AND MATS

Good picture frames are often almost as expensive as the painting itself. Oil paintings can be framed very simply by "stripping" the canvas and tacking the strips of wood (1/4-inch or 3/8-inch stock is adequate) through the canvas into the stretchers. If you cut strips from pine, walnut, or any other wood somewhat wider than the thickness of the painting, this gives it a projecting edge that neatly outlines the canvas and, through its projection over the face of the canvas, compensates for the natural unevenness of most canvas paintings. Stripping can be done by framing shops or, with some minimal tools, at home. For prints, drawings, and etchings it is possible to buy simple wooden frames in art supply stores. Most of these stores will accept special size orders without much extra charge. The straight frames, not too heavy and

Painting with "strip" frame.

without fancy molding cuts, are not only the cheapest but usually the best quality. Many stores carry these frames in oak, which can be naturally finished or painted. Then you will have to order a piece of glass from a local glazier and get a mat board in a suitable color and perhaps a piece of Masonite as a backing. (For smaller prints, a heavy cardboard might do.) A sharp mat knife, a straightedge, a steady hand, and patience are all you need to cut your own mats.

If you decide to buy frames for your artwork, the newer plastic and metal frames are extremely handsome. Some come in a variety of sizes or are adjustable. Metal frames, though particularly attractive for contemporary prints and graphics, are expensive.

Certain graphics—posters, for example—are quite inexpensive. They can be displayed without frames either by matting them or by mounting them on a cardboard or Masonite surface. Though the graphics will eventually fade or yellow, matting or mounting them may be an acceptable alternative to expensive framing.

SCULPTURE

It is hard to acquire original sculpture on a budget, but the route suggested for paintings—young artists, art schools, or community art exhibitions—can lead you to some reasonably priced, worthwhile pieces. It is possible to find interesting old sculpture for reasonable prices in antique stores or at auctions. Sometimes objects such as carved newel posts or parts of demolished buildings—which strictly speaking were not meant to be sculpture—can be successful as sculptural pieces in homes. You might also use objects from nature, such as rocks or wood formations, as sculptural elements.

While most residential interiors do not have enough space for more than one or two major pieces of sculpture, a single piece, properly displayed and

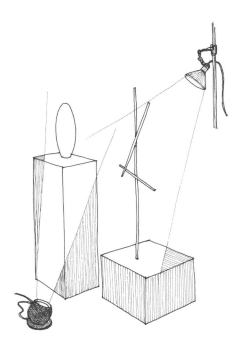

Ways of displaying and lighting sculpture.

well lit, can be a great design feature. If you have a piece of sculpture in need of a base or not tall enough to be seen at eye level, you can make a pedestal from plywood. Painting such pedestals in flat black or white provides the best background for most sculptural objects, and a small spotlight standing on the floor, or attached to the edge of a bookshelf, to a tall object, or to the ceiling, can provide a handsome and dramatic setting. Small pieces of sculpture can be displayed on any surface or shelf but should be balanced like any other art object and should usually have enough space around them to permit viewing from at least three sides.

NONCONVENTIONAL ART

Whether we call certain objects *art, crafts,* or any other name is a question of semantics. Many people collect and display objects which to others might not be art. Often these personal statements are precisely the elements which make their homes unique. It may take courage and sophistication to use a beautifully molded piece of plastic from a package as a wall hanging or to display a fascinating object which was made as a sewer brush; but if you like the form of "found" things, there is no reason why they cannot be used.

Fabrics can be highly decorative, and some contemporary prints, especially, can make large wall hangings as effective as old tapestries. Good photographs are works of art, of course. Maps and charts, particularly old maps, are often decorative and beautiful. Since many old maps come out of books, their prices are quite low. Illustrations from old books (or from new books) are another source for inexpensive graphic material. By rummaging through some used-book stores, you might be able to find something of interst to you—possibly even a whole set of illustrations that can be matted and framed.

Folk art is the generic term for simple, inexpensive, traditional objects made by artists/craftsmen in many countries. South American folk art, although often produced in large quantities in commercial enterprises, still has great charm. Folk art or "primitive" art, from Africa to Asia to our own American regional crafts, is almost always inexpensive. Antique shops, junk shops, and flea markets are good sources for a vast variety of art objects. Whether you like large three-dimensional letters from an old sign, perhaps a sign originally painted as an advertisement, or a stained glass window salvaged from a Victorian house is a matter of choice. Old tools and primitive implements, too, have much decorative value.

Although I have said that there is no need to hang something on every or any wall, and warned that no art is better than bad art, I do believe that art, crafts, and objects of personal interest can do much to enhance any interior. One of the best ways to transform an anonymous space into an interesting, personal one is through the intelligent and sensitive use of art. The design quality is not determined by the amount of money spent but by the choice of objects and by the way they are displayed.

25/ Plants

Indoor plants are one of the most attractive and least expensive design features to be found. Plants can be more than simply an afterthought in planning a room; they can be the major design statement.

Just about every plant is beautiful in itself. When you select plants, try to evaluate the shape and scale, as well as the textural quality, of each individual plant as well as of any combination you want to group together. Some plants are sculptural and dynamic in form. Others are quiet and serene. Their growth patterns vary. If you place three or four plants together, and after some time they all turn into fairly large, treelike plants, the chances are that they will compete visually with one another and with other things in the room.

The only plants that do not measure up to our design criteria are artificial ones. Plants need care, and not every plant will survive in every setting, but artificial plants and flowers have no place in a well-designed home. I have stressed honesty of materials and truth in form and structure as key considerations in evaluating design. Since nature can never be copied perfectly, even the most faithful reproduction of a plant is bound to be a dismal failure.

The best location for plants is near sunny windows. The temptation to use plants or trees away from windows, as pure design elements or as room dividers, is often doomed. There are special lamps for growing plants indoors, but it is complicated and costly to depend entirely upon artificial light. However, if your home is on the dark side, such devices might be the only way

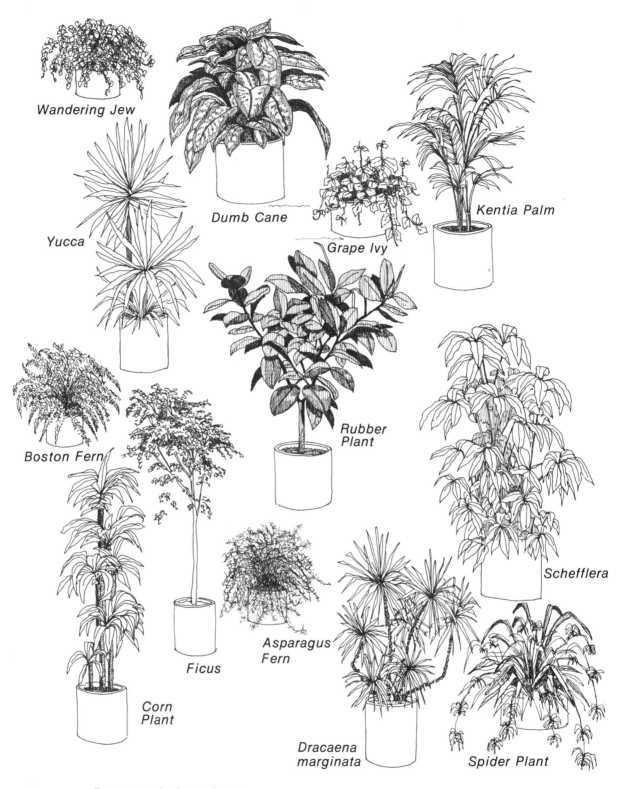

Easy-care indoor plants

to have some indoor plants. Plants do not need any special setting. One, two, or three plants sitting on the floor near a window are splendid. Ordinary clay pots are cheaper and better looking than plastic ones. If you can find some ceramic ones for reasonable prices, so much the better; but it is not necessary to spend money on elaborate pots.

If you have enough space and sunlight, a collection of plants set into a special area, perhaps defined with a border and filled with pebbles, can be a major design feature (see p. 53). Another excellent arrangement has already been mentioned in connection with window treatments and is illustrated on page 88—it consists of shelving installed over a window area for a variety of potted plants. The use of hanging plants is particularly attractive, whether singly or with other plants. It provides exciting forms and patterns at a height that normally lacks decorative elements (see p. 42). Try using several hanging plants in one area at different heights. Most plaster ceilings are strong enough to hold the weight of normal plants and require only ordinary screw eyes. If your ceiling is made of sheetrock or if the plaster is brittle, you might have to use a toggle bolt or similar device for installation.

Recent years have seen an enormous growth in the popularity of indoor plants, and as a result you can find many shops, many choices, and budget-range prices. Many plant shops carry inexpensive pots, hangers, and decorative ropes, and most will give free advice on which plants do well in various locations. A word of warning about some of the accessories sold in plant shops: special devices for the display of plants—for example, floor-to-ceiling tension poles with adjustable shelves—tend to be badly designed furniture items. It is best to use plants without elaborate trappings. Any of the arrangements I have suggested are better and cheaper than the commercial devices sold in stores.

A few plants are illustrated here; these are plants that do well in interiors and are not expensive. The costs vary from region to region and availability is sometimes seasonal. One of the cheapest ways to acquire plants is to propagate them yourself. I have no "green thumb," but I have succeeded in growing large grapefruit trees from grapefruit pits, and I have had equally good luck with avocado plants. This way to save money can also be fun; there's great satisfaction in growing plants and watching them thrive.

Fresh flowers add real sparkle and color and are an even better decorative touch in many interiors, but since they do not last long they cannot be classified as "inexpensive" in the sense that plants can.

26/Flooring

Many people feel compelled to install new flooring or carpeting as soon as they move into a new home. Since flooring is a major investment, that decision is often the first, and most serious, mistake they make. In apartments, and even in many private homes, your best bet is to consider carefully all the alternatives before rushing into carpeting or other new flooring.

Flooring in apartment buildings is either wood or tile. Older apartments and older homes almost invariably have wooden floors, with the exception of kitchens and bathrooms. The most common is oak strip flooring. Very old homes, especially in rural areas, may have fir strip floors, and luxury apartment houses may have parquet floors in the major living spaces. In rowhouses or brownstone houses, you might even find a perfectly beautiful wooden floor under several layers of linoleum; and if you live in a very old building, you might even find wide planks, which restore beautifully.

Wooden floors can easily be refinished, even if they are in bad shape. You can have them sanded down commercially, or you can rent a floor sander for a day and do it yourself (it is dusty and dirty work, but not difficult). After floors are sanded down, they must be refinished. Even if the floors do not have to be stripped completely, they may require a new finish. There are a number of excellent products available for this purpose but they are not cheap. The polyurethane floor finishes are so strong and impervious to stain and abrasion that they are about as maintenance-free as any tile. These are available in dull and glossy finishes; the dull or satin finish usually looks best. It is also easy to stain wood floors; the natural light color of oak or hardwood floors is not the only possibility. Penetrating wood stains come in many different shades, from light brown to mahogany and dark walnut. A medium-dark or dark stained floor can look much richer than a natural oak-colored floor and can enhance a lighter-colored area rug. Since wood is a natural and warm material, it is popular in furniture and wall paneling. Surprisingly enough, many fine wooden floors are covered at great expense with carpeting and wood paneling has then been installed at further cost! I think that existing wooden floors represent the best possible background for most rooms and that covering such floors is a poor idea.

A wooden floor in an eating space is easier to maintain than carpeting. Even floors that are not treated with polyurethane or vinyl finishes can easily be cleaned if any food is spilled. Likewise, a wooden floor in a child's room can be maintained almost as conveniently as tile or linoleum, especially if properly treated with one of the protective coatings or with wax.

I have suggested area rugs for living spaces, and I repeat here that they are not only cheaper than wall-to-wall carpet but last longer, too: they can be rotated for wear and moved to other homes. Obviously, however, wall-to-wall carpeting has a number of advantages: it can visually unify spaces that are broken up and busy; it requires nothing but vacuuming for maintenance; and it provides a feeling of luxury underfoot. The luxury is particularly desirable in sleeping areas. My preference for area rugs is based on cost-saving factors, above all. If you decide to use wall-to-wall carpeting, the cheapest is unfortunately not always the best buy. Whether the cost breakdown is stated or not, you are paying for the cost of padding and installation, in addition to the actual carpeting. If you pay below $10 per square yard installed, it is quite likely that the padding and installation represents about one-third of the cost; your terrific bargain might be such cheap merchandise that it will last no more than a couple of years. Good carpeting, under normal wear, should last for at least eight years.

Whatever the fiber, the cost is determined by the pile height, the ply of the yarn, and the number of face yarns per inch. If you purchase carpeting from a reliable dealer you will most likely get a fair value. Discount stores have continuous sales of cheap goods, which might be fine for limited use but should be carefully considered if you are buying carpeting as a permanent investment. Many excellent synthetic fibers are used for carpeting, and there a number of conventional weaves (Wilton, Velvet, Axminster, Chenille), as well as newer ones, such as machine tufting.

The most luxurious and beautiful material is still wool; it is also the most expensive. There are beautiful weaves, subtle colors, and handsome textures in wool, synthetic fibers, and cotton; there are just as many (or more) poor colors, busy patterns, and tortured textures. Your choice of carpeting will depend upon the appearance, the durability, and the price. For durability, traffic areas should not be carpeted with high-piled textures, since they tend to mat down. High pile is very pleasant in a bedroom, and it is certainly a good choice for a small area rug. You might consider so-called commercial carpeting, although the better varieties are often as expensive as any residential carpeting. Good commercial carpeting is designed for specification by architects and designers, who tend to reject the busy and gaudy patterns and textures made for the general public. The soft beiges and subtle grays frequently used for offices are equally beautiful in living spaces. They take extremely heavy wear and are suggested for stairs for that reason.

I have mentioned indoor-outdoor carpeting in connection with bathrooms and carpet tiles when I discussed playrooms. Indoor-outdoor carpeting is not luxurious, but it is reasonably priced and can be installed by the layman. Where the floors are in very bad shape, where the only existing flooring is concrete, or where some ugly tiles have been used, it could be a good choice. It can also be used in bathrooms and kitchens. A number of carpets are made on rubber backing and can be installed as easily as indoor-outdoor carpeting. Again, these are not luxurious or particularly well designed, but they will fit into most budgets. Sisal carpeting and tiles have long been popular in other countries and are becoming more so here. Sisal flooring is very handsome and can last for many, many years. If that idea appeals to you, you might have to shop around a bit. It is considerably cheaper than ordinary carpeting and since it is a natural material, usually quite beautiful. A number of hemp carpets (made from a grass variety) are now available, as are rope and jute carpets; they are similar to sisal in price and durability and are also very handsome. Even Tatami mats (the standard Japanese floor covering) can be used successfully in our homes, but they do require careful treatment (such as removing one's shoes).

Area rugs come in any size, quality, and design, from simple cotton throw rugs to handwoven Oriental rugs. As long as your furniture is either on the rug or off the rug, the size can be determined by seating groups or any other space that you'd like to define; a 6- by 9-foot rug might be just large enough for a living space. For that reason the quality of an area rug can be much higher than wall-to-wall carpeting, for which 30 or 40 square yards might be required. Besides the Scandinavian rugs, many other domestic and imported rugs are appropriate and inexpensive. Depending upon the textures and colors that you plan to use, a high-pile Greek "flokati" (sheep's hair) rug might be the right choice, or a deep pile soft wool rug, or even an Oriental rug. Orientals range from very costly, old, handwoven ones, to machine-made inexpensive ones. Since the real ones are so much more beautiful than the imitations, you might find a used Oriental rug within your budget. Their construction is so strong that they can last for many decades under continuous use. Chinese rugs are as beautiful and durable as Oriental rugs but equally difficult to find for budget prices. Braided rugs are available at reasonable cost, but they are not always appropriate in contemporary interiors. Solid-colored, textured area rugs are often beautiful. You can get a good buy by ordering a piece of regular high-pile luxury carpeting in the right size and having it bound and seamed by the dealer. A 6- by 9-foot rug, for instance, is just 6 square yards. Even if you select a really expensive wool rug and add the cost of binding and seaming, the total cost is still within reason and possibly quite a bit less than a "designed," readymade area rug. And if you want to achieve the same at very low cost, purchase remnants or ends of broadloom rolls.

I am concentrating on carpeting and rugs as new or added floor coverings, since most other materials tend to be costly. However, tile and linoleum can be considered within a limited price range. Solid vinyl tile or sheet material is very expensive and, I believe, overrated. For kitchens, playrooms, children's rooms, workrooms, and possibly bathrooms, vinyl asbestos tile is adequate and much cheaper than sheet vinyl. Asphalt tile is the least expensive resilient floor covering, and it will serve you well for workrooms, bathrooms, and other spaces that need a new permanent floor covering. Linoleum and other sheet materials in similar compositions are marketed in a vast array of poor designs and fake patterns, and you will have to search carefully to find attractive designs. It is easier to find designs you like among tiles. Perhaps the most attractive tiles or sheet vinyls are those in solid colors, although they are somewhat more difficult to maintain since they show scuff marks and spots more obviously than patterned flooring.

Permanent or semipermanent installation should be avoided. The moment you decide to rip out the existing floor covering and start from scratch, a major portion of your budget will be committed. If your apartment has tile floors, you can probably achieve a very acceptable effect with some area rugs. If you live in a very old house with wooden floors beyond restoration, you might consider paint. In fact, some deck paints and epoxy paints will adhere to just about any surface, including concrete and tile. Painted floors can be quite attractive and colorful and represent one of the cheapest floor solutions.

Ceramic or quarry tile, slate, marble, or stone—while all most attractive—are out of the question for any home designed with budget limitations. If your home already has any of these permanent more structural or architectural materials, by all means take advantage of them.

Since color, texture, and pattern are very much related to the total space that you are dealing with, it is impossible to make specific suggestions about floor colors and patterns. In case of doubt, soft, subdued, and neutral colors are easier to work with than very bright, intense colors or busy patterns. Lighter colors, especially in carpeting, are easier to maintain than dark colors. Black carpeting is just about the most difficult since every speck of dust or lint will show.

To save money, often the most sensible approach is to work with the existing flooring, unless it is totally unacceptable. Of the many design elements that make up an interior, the cost of new flooring can be the highest. Beginning to economize literally from the floor up seems a sure way of staying within your budget.

27/Wall Coverings

Many interiors are far better off with their natural walls and surfaces than with wall coverings. This is a word of warning before you rush out to buy expensive wallpapers, which may detract from a well-designed space.

By nature, wall coverings are an added and literally superficial element in interior design. Every wall is a material in itself; ideally, no material need be covered up. There are very elegant and expensive modern interiors which use exposed concrete walls to great advantage. Undoubtedly, certain inexpensive structural materials such as cement block walls are not the epitome of comfort, beauty, and warmth; but even they are probably superior to a wall which has been pasted over with brick-patterned wallpaper or some such. The walls in many older buildings have been covered and pasted over many times. Sometimes the original wall surface is far superior to the many layers of added materials. In fact, if you live in an old building with a brick wall underneath, you might find it worth the effort to strip the plaster off the walls. A natural brick wall, even if old and uneven, can easily become the strongest asset in an interior. Or you might even uncover handsome wood paneling or wainscoting.

It is difficult to design a room which is dominated by a strong design, pattern, or color on all wall surfaces. It is somewhat easier to create interesting and flexible spaces if paper is used on one or two walls only, or perhaps just on the ceiling. I have already mentioned the decorative possibilities of carefully selected accent areas for wallpaper in such specific places as children's rooms, bathrooms, or entry areas.

Of course, there are many very beautiful wall coverings, but I think it important first to consider what they are. The wall covering used most often in residential interiors is wallpaper. Decorative wallpapers have been used for centuries, and some of the early Oriental papers are true works of art, created by artists. Most commercial papers marketed today are mass-produced and have little artistic quality when they try to imitate old motifs or murals. There are, however, some very exciting and decorative contemporary papers.

Some of the nicest wallpapers are made of natural materials, such as Oriental grass cloth or shiki silk. Unfortunately, they are quite expensive. Wall coverings made of fabrics and fibers laminated to paper backing are also available in linen, straw, and burlap textures. The last especially is quite inexpensive, and sometimes is made with a protective plastic coating for easy maintenance. These textured wall coverings present several advantages. They do have acoustical (sound-absorbing) qualities; they are fairly thick and therefore can cover cracks and bumps on old or poor plaster surfaces; and they provide a pleasant, subtle textural background for the other furnishings. One of the best and cheapest wall coverings is canvas, sometimes sold as painters' canvas. It is not recommended as a decorative or textural wall covering, but it is an excellent material for walls that are beyond repair. Since canvas is quite strong, it can be used literally to hold together crumbling plaster; it is heavy enough to equalize bumps and cracks. Most other fabric wall coverings, whether laminated to paper backing or used directly on walls, are fairly costly. Soft coverings like felt have very good acoustical properties, and felt coverings, suede, or vinyl suedes provide a luxurious visual effect. Better wallpaper stores carry felt and suede laminated to paper backing; indeed, almost any fabric can be laminated to paper backing for ease of installation. The cost of these wall coverings is unfortunately rather high. The vinyl felts and vinyl suedes are more reasonable and offer easy maintenance.

Wallpaper patterns are strongly influenced by fashion, and each year new ones appear for certain "looks." In recent years, the "wet look" was quite popular; shiny and glossy papers or vinyls, often in really bright colors, were used extensively. They were not sensible investments since they were expensive and the fashion was rather short-lived. As always, choose what you want to live with, not what the decorating magazines dictate.

Vinyl wall coverings, especially fabric-backed ones, are often good and lasting surfacing materials. Although the initial cost is higher than for ordinary wallpapers, good vinyls are so strong that they can last for many years, in kitchens, bathrooms, or other areas which get hard wear and much scrubbing.

If you choose any wall covering, you should be clear about your criteria. If you need a material because the walls in your home are bad, or because you wish to avoid repeated painting, you are probably better off with a simple texture or a very small pattern or design. A good-quality wall covering should last; if it is a plain texture, the chances are that you will not tire of it, and it can be the backdrop for whatever you like to display—artwork, plants, collections. If you select a paper purely for color, design, or as a fun accent, you will most likely feel like changing it after a couple of years, and for that reason using the paper on a limited wall surface, rather than for a whole room or apartment, would be wise. Lastly, you might keep in mind that plain or textured wall covering can be painted over, whereas strong designs and colors are difficult to cover.

Papers known as "contact paper" are not really meant to be used as permanent wall coverings. They come with their own adhesive backing and are difficult to apply on large surfaces without forming bubbles. They do not stand up as well as papers mounted with regular wallpaper paste, and therefore the decision to use contact papers because they do not require a professional paper hanger is probably a mistake. There are preglued wallpapers you can install yourself.

A really good buy to consider is cork. There are cork tiles, and there is cork as sheet material. The least expensive is Portuguese cork—originally used as insulation for refrigeration purposes, this is now available in sheet or tile form, as thin as 3/8 inch. It is very reasonably priced when bought by the carton and can be glued to walls without much difficulty. It makes an excellent accent wall, has good acoustic qualities, and can be used to tack up posters or drawings. The edges are very brittle, and you must be sure to protect them all either by applying the cork wall-to-wall or by finishing off the edges with some kind of molding strip.

If you are handy, you can also obtain large sheet materials in lumber yards, which sometimes have to be installed on furring strips, much like wood paneling. (Furring strips are needed to level the wall surfaces and provide nailing strips. For cork tiles this is not necessary, since the tiles are flexible enough to bend over uneven surfaces and are glued rather than nailed.) One inexpensive material is "Homasote," a very plain fiber board, usually made in gray. It is easy to paint, and it takes nails and tacks extremely well; in fact, it is used quite frequently on walls of art galleries or exhibition areas. A similar material is fiber board, which comes in a variety of thicknesses and strengths, from the consistency of Masonite to rather soft, untreated paper fibers. These two materials are cheaper than plywood or solid wood but require about the same expertise for application. The fact that they are not finished allows for a more personal design treatment; and the extra work involved is compensated for by a much lower cost.

A book devoted to good design at low cost might conceivably not have mentioned wall coverings at all. Their use should be carefully considered; if not really necessary, painting the existing walls is often the better solution.

28/ Paint/ Finishes

WALLS

Paint is the least expensive, and often the most desirable, wall finish. Professional painters are not usually too expensive; students and handymen often do a competent job; and for those who wish to undertake their own painting, loads of information and advice is available through paint stores, instruction manuals, and do-it-yourself books.

Getting the color you really want can be a problem for the apartment dweller; landlords often restrict what they'll do for the new tenant. If you want a particular shade try: (1) insisting on it, (2) offering to purchase your own paint, (3) offering to pay a little extra to the painters, or (4) as a last resort, settle for white everywhere and then paint over it yourself (but remember you may have to paint it back to white when you move!). If your landlord agrees to paint only one color per room, and if you wish to have an accent color on one wall or on the woodwork of a room, it will be cheapest to paint the accent wall in a different color yourself after the completion of the basic work.

White is one of the best background colors for most interiors, and contrary to popular belief, it does not show more dirt than muted colors. If you live in a heavily polluted area, white walls and white ceilings will show dirt, but so will beige, pale green, and so on. Some painters insist on tinting chalk-white paint in order to cover previous surfaces. Usually this makes sense, but if the tint turns out to be something approaching "institutional buff," insist on your own choice. Within the available range of white, off-whites, and other pale colors, there is quite a difference which you might only be able to perceive by comparisons. In other words, when selecting colors, compare charts from several manufacturers for a good range of choices.

Follow this approach in the selection of bright accent colors, too. Many paint and hardware stores have the equipment to mix paints to precise shades, based on formulas provided by manufacturers. These custom-mixed paints are only a little more expensive than premixed colors and might make a considerable difference. Since strong colors tend to look far more intense on large surfaces than on a small color chart, it might be better for you to keep hues and intensities somewhat understated. It is not a good idea to select paint colors based on a piece of fabric or carpet. Those materials have textures which absorb and reflect light differently from smooth paper or wall surfaces. Mixing paint colors requires skill and experience. A professional painter is usually able to do that, but amateurs may not always succeed.

White ceilings give the best light reflection. If you have a color on your walls, a certain amount of it will be reflected onto a white ceiling anyhow; if you want the ceiling identical to the wall colors, a tint of the wall color added to the white paint is usually enough, together with the reflected light.

In old buildings with dried or slightly decaying plaster walls, it may be necessary to spend a good deal of time preparing them for painting; in fact, spackling, repairs, sanding, and prime coats take more time than the actual final paint coat, but it is worth the effort. Surfaces which have many hairline cracks and minor blemishes can sometimes be camouflaged with sand finish paint. This has a grainy texture that can be rather attractive. If you want to paint over existing wallpaper, you must make sure that it is still firmly glued to the wall; otherwise painting may be a waste of time. It is always better to remove existing wallpaper by peeling or steaming if off, but this takes time and may be rather expensive when done professionally. In new buildings it is usually a good idea to have all the walls painted, even if you plan to have certain areas papered later. All new construction will settle somewhat, and cracks may not develop until some time after you have moved in. Also, contractors seem to do a better job preparing and spackling new surfaces if they are to be painted rather than papered.

The quality of paint varies considerably from grade to grade and manufacturer to manufacturer. It may be wise to select a fairly good-quality paint rather than the cheapest brand available. A number of paints are made to do particular jobs. Latex paints are easier to handle than oil-based paints. In general, flat paints are the preferred finishes for interiors. Several manufacturers make flat enamels, which can be washed and maintained easily; they do not have the sheen of glossy or semigloss paints. Glossy paints can be used to great advantage in spaces other than kitchens and bathrooms, but this requires very good wall and ceiling surfaces. Sometimes exciting results can be achieved with rooms painted completely in glossy dark paints, although this decorative feat requires courage and probably a good deal of experience. Your local paint store will be able to help you choose the appropriate type and quality for your purposes.

FURNITURE AND WOODWORK

There are countless ways to finish shelving, built-in furniture, and old furniture. Among the best and cheapest for good-quality woodwork is an oil finish. This finish requires a smooth, well-sanded surface and is suitable for hardwoods only. Rough lumber or fir plywood cannot be treated effectively by oiling. Walnut, teak, maple, oak, and mahogany are examples of hardwood, and for either solid wood or veneered surfaces only boiled linseed oil is required (every hardware store carries linseed oil; very inexpensive). The oil should be applied by rubbing it firmly with a soft rag into the wood in the direction of the grain. After the first coat has dried, repeat the process several times, each time making sure that the oil is properly rubbed in and that the surface does not look wet. Oil brings out the natural beauty of wood grain better than any other wood finish or varnish, but it does tend to darken it. An oil finish has the further advantage of easy maintenance. Once a surface has been finished, a new oil rubbing should be applied after several months and repeated from time to time. That way the wood has a protective film and will stand up well against rings, water spots, or food spills. A similar but somewhat less permanent finish is wax.

Most other wood finishes, such as varnish, lacquer, and shellac, require professional knowledge and spray equipment. However, a number of oil-based products, some of them mixed with other materials, are made for the do-it-yourselfer, and most of these are as simple to handle as linseed oil. When refinishing old furniture, especially pieces that have been stripped, you may find that a residue of the old finish remains. In that case a darker finish may be necessary to blend the old and the new. Oil stains can be mixed with linseed oil, or the entire piece might be stained with a penetrating oil stain before its final finish coat. A somewhat unorthodox but workable method of dealing with old furniture makes use of the former finish. Most old pieces must be thoroughly cleaned. Doing this with very fine steel wool and turpentine will actually loosen up some of the finish and even out faded areas, giving a renewed finish to the piece while cleaning the surface dirt that has accumulated over the years.

Inexpensive plywood or soft woods may have to be painted unless they are of high quality. Special paints are recommended for wood; the kind of flat paint used on walls will not stand up well, nor will it look smooth and even. A good paint job on wood will require more than one application and some sanding or steel wooling in between coats. Really bright colors in paint and lacquer offer good potential for decorative treatments, especially on beat-up furniture or ancient kitchen cabinets. Basically, on good wood I would recommend finishes which do not obliterate the grain and beauty of the material. Paint may be the easy answer, but it takes a great deal of effort to remove it. Many old homes have had coat after coat of paint applied to handsome woodwork, and you might be the new owner who is forced to dedicate hours of work to restoring the woodwork to its original appearance.

For small surfaces or for metal, spray paint is fast and does not require brushes and other paraphernalia. It is, however, very expensive when used for larger areas.

LAMINATES

The best-known laminates are plastic ones such as Formica or Micarta, which stand up to just about any normal wear, are waterproof and stain-proof, and make excellent work or eating surfaces. Unless you are very handy, it is not a good idea to resurface an existing piece of furniture or to finish something that you are building with plastic laminates. If you are experienced in woodworking, be sure to purchase the proper adhesive and to follow the instructions exactly. Plastic laminates are much more expensive than natural or painted finishes, but they are worthwhile for heavily used surfaces. Some local lumber yards with shop facilities, and sometimes a local cabinetmaker, can be found who can make up laminated tops at reasonable prices. The best designs are the solid colors. Although everybody, including manufacturers of well-designed furniture, uses wood-grained plastic laminates, none of these imitation patterns comes up to the appearance of the more honest solid colors.

Less well-known possibilities for laminations exist; for instance, linoleum can be glued to wood fairly simply, and cork or tempered Masonite can make good surfaces. For old cabinets or closet doors you might even consider 1/4-inch veneered plywood, but the fastening process requires a certain amount of skill. Oilcloth, available in drafting supply or art stores, can be a very serviceable surface; it can be cut and wrapped like ordinary paper. Many architects use oilcloth covers on their drafting tables and get many years of use.

With the exception of oilcloth, all laminates need some kind of treatment for the edges. Plastic laminates are very thin and can easily be "self-edged." For materials such as linoleum, you will probably need solid wood edges to trim off surfaces.

For little-used doors and for surfaces such as the inside of closets or cabinets, fabric wrapping is a relatively easy finishing process. Any fabric from velvet to plastic can be cut and wrapped carefully around thin sheets of Masonite or plywood, then tacked to a surface. That technique can make your old closet doors attractive design features and the inside of a beat-up storage or display case quite elegant.

When you are faced with decisions about walls, about furniture, about woodwork or surfaces, it always pays to explore the ways and means of restoring rather than attempting to start again. For old buildings or furnishings, the original finish was usually the right one. If you live in a new building or you have purchased new furniture, it might be wisest to make the best use of what there is, without trying to create a new "make-believe" finish or surfacing.

29/Fabrics

The vast variety of fabrics available makes selection often difficult and confusing. This is simplified somewhat for us since the choice of high-quality budget-priced fabrics is limited. The fact that many upholstery goods run to over $50 per yard does not mean that costly fabrics are greatly superior. The high price tag is often for handwoven material, for complicated designs and weaves, and for the prestigious name attached to the material.

Budget-priced furniture is most often marketed with a preselected choice of cover material in a graded series of quality. Again, the choice here is simpler than attempting to select upholstery from the practically unlimited sources available in fabric stores and showrooms. The price of a sofa or chair in most retail stores includes the cover. In wholesale showrooms, the price is given "in muslin," which covers the cost of labor for upholstery but not the cost of the actual material. You must be careful in this situation, since a reasonably priced sofa may become very expensive indeed if 16 yards of upholstery fabric at $15 or $20 per yard is added to the purchase price. If you buy inexpensive upholstered pieces, the lowest grade of fabric might not be the wisest choice. The quality of upholstery fabric greatly determines the maintenance and the lasting appearance of a piece of furniture. A slightly higher initial investment for a stronger, better fabric is usually a good idea.

Textile fibers are either natural or man-made. The common natural fibers are cotton, linen, wool, and silk. *Silk* is expensive, does not wear well, and is not recommended for budget interiors. *Cotton* and *linen* are made from vegetable fibers. Both are durable and pliable; in their natural state they are also very handsome. Unless they are interwoven (mixed) with other fibers, they are usually not sturdy enough for upholstery use, but they are excellent as curtains, spreads, and throws. However, some cottons (Haitian cotton, for example) are very heavy, and some of the linen fabrics are made in heavy weight. If you want to use them, be sure that they are specifically recommended for upholstery. *Wool* is an animal fiber and is usually considerably more expensive than cotton or linen. Despite the enormous competition from synthetics, the quality, touch, and appearance of wool still make it the best and most beautiful of the upholstery fabrics. If you can get solid or textured woolen fabrics for a reasonable price—perhaps a remnant on sale, or perhaps the somewhat higher grade of choices available for standard upholstery—it will probably be an excellent design selection, and it will stand up well for many years.

Man-made fabrics are marketed under many trade names (such as Antron for E. I. Du Pont's nylon, or Kodel for Eastman Kodak's polyester) but consist of a relatively small number of generic fabrics.

Glass fibers (*fiber glass*) are woven into many weaves from sheer to heavy textures. They are easy to care for, fireproof, and inexpensive. But the touch, or "hand," of the fabric is not very pleasant, and the appearance is not up to that of natural fibers. *Acetate* is made by a number of companies under various trade names, but it is usually combined with rayon or cotton. Its "hand" is pleasant, but it needs more care and maintenance than fiber glass. *Acrylic* is probably the man-made fabric closest to wool in appearance and feel. It is best known under the trade name of Acrilan (Chemstrand Corporation), but it is also made into textiles under some other trade names. Acrilan is widely used as a carpeting fiber. *Modacrylics* are modified acrylics, easy to care for, and known as flameproof fibers. *Nylon* is a hard-wearing fiber, highly suitable for home furnishings materials. While some of the inexpensive nylon fabrics have an objectionable sheen, it is possible to find good-looking and well-designed examples.

Polyester fabrics are used extensively for durable press garments, but are also used widely for curtains and bedspreads. *Rayon* is equally popular for dress fabrics and interior textiles. Most of the time rayon is used as a blend with polyesters and other synthetic fibers. *Saran* and *Spandex* are relatively new fibers in the home furnishings field. Both are easy to care for and have nonflammable qualities.

The properties of fibers in terms of fireproofing, ease of maintenance, and other industrial standard ratings are not as crucial in residential use as in the design of large-scale public and commercial interiors. It is worthwhile, however, to have the store or supplier explain to you the properties and labeling of fabrics as they relate to the Bureau of Standards classifications. Although controls exist, no textile is guaranteed by the manufacturers to last forever, to be completely fade-proof, or never to shrink. The reputable mills provide all pertinent information to the best of their knowledge, and retail stores are frequently willing to pass this information on to the consumer. Don't hesitate to ask as many questions as possible about the durability of the fabrics you are considering.

The various weaves do not determine the price nor necessarily the quality of fabrics. Three types of weaves are the most common: plain weaves, which include plain and basket weaves; pile weaves, which include both cut and uncut weaves; and floating weaves, which include twill and satin weaves. With these weaves a great variety of textures can be produced. Patterns are created through a number of printing processes or on a Jacquard loom. The complex field of textile technology produces a number of fabrics using different techniques; for instance, expanded vinyl is a popular, reasonably priced, and often well-designed upholstery material made with an elastic knit fabric backing. Felt, made of wool and a mixture of fibers, is another nonwoven fabric which can provide excellent touches of intense color on pillows or table coverings, though it is not suitable for upholstery.

Lightweight fabrics for curtains are available at low prices. The best buys for curtain materials are the open weaves, ranging in texture from fishnet to the more solidly woven casements. These fabrics come in just about any fiber, often in natural colors or white, sometimes interwoven with stripes and contrasting colors. Linen casement cloths are particularly handsome and are not expensive. Some of the synthetic net fabrics come in extra wide widths and are good buys if you plan to sew your own curtains. The standard width for curtain and upholstery fabrics is 48 to 54 inches wide, but some of the open-weave fabrics are as wide as 120 inches. Cotton and linens make excellent curtains in plain or solid colors, as do homespun fabrics (somewhat irregular weaves). Printed fabrics are more difficult to select, since the design as well as the price varies widely. India prints are durable, inexpensive, yet intricate designs printed on cotton. Another good buy in fabrics are the Mexican or South American cottons, often in lively colors, sometimes in stripes.

Medium-weight fabrics are suitable for upholstery, heavy curtains, slipcovers, bedspreads, and so on, but are not recommended for furniture that gets heavy wear. One of the long-time favorite fabrics for the budget-minded is burlap; its coarse basket weave forms a handsome texture. Not a strong fabric, it can be used for curtains or perhaps as a wall fabric. Canvas and denim are both cotton fabrics, quite firm and durable, inexpensive and well designed. They are not usually provided as a selection for standard furniture but are both good choices should you plan to reupholster existing or recycled pieces. Hopsacking, sailcloth, and duck are in the same price and quality range and can again be recommended highly. Lastly, you might consider mattress ticking as a possible upholstery material—again a durable material available in a good choice of colors and stripes.

Heavy-weight fabrics are used primarily for upholstery. They are the strongest materials, made in just about any fiber and combinations of fibers. Hardly any heavy-weight fabrics are washable. I have already mentioned plastics (vinyl) as good value for durable materials. However, plastic fabrics do not have the softness and warmth of woven fabrics, so they are not the best choice for all situations. Using a vinyl fabric on the seats of dining chairs might be an excellent idea, since they can be wiped clean. Plastic on an upholstered chair or sofa would be sticky in hot weather and might not give you the inviting appearance you hoped for. The only other heavy-weight fabric available at budget prices is corduroy, which is very durable and, unlike other heavy-weight fabrics, usually washable.

If you are concerned about long-lasting qualities, ask for "commercial" fabrics. Materials made for institutional use must take a great deal of abuse. Not only are they stronger, but since they are usually specified by professional designers and architects, they are often better designed than fabrics made for home use. Tightly woven tweeds or "transportation cloth" are good choices for furniture destined for heavy use. For these pieces, it is false economy to settle for a cheap material that will show wear after less than a year. With certain materials the cost per yard can give you a fair indication of its durability; for instance, a cotton velvet priced below $10 per yard might be handsome, but the chances are that it will not last very long. On the other hand, the more expensive velvets, velours, and plush fabrics made for theater seating stand up for long periods of time.

Many upholstery fabrics are treated with Sylmer finish, a protective coating. While treated fabrics do stand up better to dirt and spot removal, they are certainly not impervious to spots and damage. There are many maintenance factors to be considered. One of the first might be the location of your home; in polluted areas, white curtains will soil and therefore your choice should be a washable fabric. In a family with small children, a light-colored velvet on dining chairs will not stay clean for long. And if you plan to spend every evening sitting in a particular favorite chair, that chair should get a really strong upholstery material in order to last.

A word about stores: if there is a "mill end" or fabric discount store in your area, you can probably find excellent buys there. If you do not need much yardage, many department stores feature remnant tables where good buys can be found, and some towns have special "remnant stores." Quite frequently fabric distributors or wholesale houses run sales which are open to the public. After you have figured your exact needs, it certainly pays to spend some time shopping around. The market is competitive and prices can vary widely from store to store.

30/ The Market

Shopping for good design on a budget is a challenge in a consumer-oriented society. It is essential to survey the market and to eliminate products of poor quality from consideration. But it is also important to search out the good sources.

WHOLESALE

Most budget-priced furnishings are available through retail outlets. The wholesale market does not always offer the bargains it appears to, but it is possible at times to find good buys through wholesale sources. Many wholesale showrooms and distributors are restricted by trade laws to selling only to retailers who stock their merchandise. Many other excellent sources also offer their products only through the services of decorators, designers, and architects; although they usually have good-quality merchandise and high design standards, they are expensive. Most of these wholesale houses are "trade" showrooms exclusively and never sell their merchandise at retail. Their list prices are therefore somewhat misleading and frequently highly inflated. Even with the designers' discount, much of the home furnishings merchandise marketed this way is out of range for the budget-minded. Unless you have a helpful friend who is a design professional, probably the absolute net or wholesale price will not be available to you. You must also consider the fact that wholesale establishments charge for delivery (included in the purchase price by most retailers). Of course, trade or wholesale houses offer many services that you cannot get from retailers. Samples are freely available; also unlimited choice of colors and sizes, and changes or modifications, are possible for furniture, carpeting, wall surfacings, and fabrics. In addition, photographs or illustrations of possible choices, carefully written "memos" for prices, different finishes on furniture, and many other special services are standard.

A number of firms exist whose method of selling is officially described as wholesale but which in reality cater directly to the consumer. Undoubtedly some provide excellent products and good service, but a good many use high-pressure sales techniques and somewhat questionable business practices. Included in these practices are introductory cards or business cards, quite readily available through some retail stores or decorators, which give the consumer the feeling that he has received special privileges to purchase at wholesale costs. A number of these firms will then transmit a commission on sales (usually 10 percent) to the dealer who referred the customer to them. While this is a perfectly legal practice, it must be pointed out that the value obtained is certainly not a wholesale price. If you find a well-designed product in such a firm, you may get a fair value, but not a fantastic bargain.

DEPARTMENT STORES

Most department stores throughout the country are well established—often they are old firms, many of them part of a larger group of stores, and most of them honest, fair, and consumer-oriented. The prices the consumer pays in department stores is determined by a combination of factors which include large overhead, advertising costs, and the stores' ability to purchase quantities of merchandise at discount costs. In other words, the prices are fair but rarely exceptional bargains.

Some department stores have major furniture, fabrics, floor covering, and wall covering departments. The managers of these departments are often perceptive, design-oriented buyers who give progressive ideas a chance. If you have the choice of more than one department store in your area, look for the one with major home furnishings promotions, exhibitions, and special sales.

Since department stores purchase in large quantities, their warehouses are often overstocked, and the sales are real, not fictitious ones. Sometimes it pays to select certain furnishings and wait patiently until the next sale before placing your order. A number of department stores also run warehouse sales, where you might find excellent buys; however, the choice is always limited, and sometimes the goods are slightly damaged.

An advantage of department stores is the service which is part of their usual operation. Delivery is almost always included in the purchase price. If an item you have bought should arrive damaged, it is relatively easy to get service or exchange, or at times an adjustment in the price.

Gaining acquaintance with what is on the market and doing some comparison shopping is very worthwhile; by starting with a store with a good reputation, you will have a solid basis for comparing less expensive products.

FURNITURE STORES

Most major furniture stores carry a variety of products in addition to furniture. Some cities and smaller towns have reputable, old furniture stores, often tradition-bound and rarely catering to people on a budget. Likewise, most areas also have sleazy furniture shops that sell "suites" of furniture ("a whole living room set of 7 pieces for only $199.95") and offer installment plan payment terms full of hidden loopholes.

Since the 1950s, certain furniture stores have carried design-conscious products at extremely reasonable prices. Many of these stores have a number of branches, and quite a few are large enough to manufacture their own products or to import a particular line. Although some of their merchandise might be "knock-offs," not quite acceptable to the professional designer, other items may be original designs.

These stores advertise in newspapers, and it is almost impossible to miss hearing about them in any part of the country. Recently, surveying the national availability of low-cost, good design furnishings, I noticed that almost every weekend edition of the larger newspapers carries some ads with illustrations and prices.

FURNITURE SPECIALTIES

Good sources for special items of furniture can be found in most larger cities. There are stores that carry furniture in parts, unpainted furniture, shelving systems and storage units, or nothing but chairs. You have to be willing and able to assemble the furniture sold in "kits," but since this system cuts down much on factory labor as well as shipping costs, the price savings can be substantial. The design quality of furniture-in-parts is often decided by the purchaser, and those pieces that must simply be put together according to instructions are usually well designed.

Stores that carry shelving systems and storage components vary widely in their design criteria. Fortunately for us, the more expensive systems are often the ugly ones; simple handsome shelving or storage components have been dressed up with elaborate decorations—almost always poor ones. Avoid these, and stick to the straightforward ones if you want good design.

Unfinished furniture can qualify as a good buy in well-designed products. Although unpainted furniture is basically made to be painted, if the wood is well sanded and has no major blemishes, a simple oil or lacquer finish can be applied; if the piece is made of hardwood, just a couple of coats of wax may be a sufficient finish. Consider unpainted furniture for children's rooms, for a handsome storage system for a bedroom, or for use in any other location in your home.

After you have surveyed the market, you may find that highly specialized stores featuring nothing but chairs or marble tables or steel and glass tables or leather-upholstered furniture will be the best sources for specific items that you have decided upon. These special stores are usually found only in large urban areas, and if you live in a major city they should certainly be on your list.

MAIL ORDER

City dwellers rarely consider mail-order firms, but the discriminating shopper can find some remarkably good buys in their catalogs. It is essential that you have a clear idea of what you are looking for and that you examine the catalog very carefully before ordering. Some furniture is quite acceptable, as are some fabrics, carpeting, and a variety of home furnishings products. In addition to the large mail-order houses, you can find advertisements for a number of small "direct-mail" or mail-order companies, and again certain special products (rugs, some chairs, small occasional tables, etc.) of good design can be discovered.

GIFT SHOPS

The only gift shops that would carry well-designed products are the rather elegant and expensive ones. Don't be discouraged by a store's reputation for high prices and luxury items, however; they usually have a number of objects and some furnishings that are reasonably priced. The better the store, the better the chances of finding well-designed objects. There are several national "good design"-type stores, as well as many individual shops, which carry tableware, glass, accessories, and furnishings. If you have consciously observed design qualities, you will recognize these stores as clearly apart from the run-of-the-mill gift store carrying useless gadgetry. In fact, the kinds of stores to be avoided are: souvenir shops, shops that have permanent "going-out-of-business" signs, and stores featuring "genuine" Oriental rugs for $15.95 apiece.

Many communities have Oriental import stores, which carry excellent buys in baskets, bedspreads, dishes, and a whole range of products. Corny decorations, cheap imitations, and gadgetry are often sold alongside the well-designed items, so you may have to pick and choose carefully. A fairly good indicator of the quality of a store's products can be the design and quality of its dishes and glassware. If it features handsome china, stoneware, or pottery, the chances are that there are other worthwhile things. If, however, the store features sets of china for eight persons for a ridiculously low price—watch out. And if the window display includes cameras for $2.95 alongside glassware, Oriental rugs, and watches, don't bother to go in.

SPECIALTY STORES

Along with "good design" furniture stores, many special lighting stores have emerged over the past years. The contemporary lighting stores tend to sell well-designed lighting devices, which are often good values. This is not the case in stores featuring expensive, old-fashioned lamps with elaborate shades and overdecorated bases. The contemporary lighting stores are like the low-cost contemporary furniture stores in their selection of well-known or "name designer" products at prices considerably lower than those of distributors carrying the original designs.

A final word about some general problems in marketing home furnishings, and especially furniture, might be useful and help prevent frustrations and disappointments.

A sizable part of the cost of any piece of furniture is its shipping cost. In fact, the shipping of raw materials to the factory, the distribution of materials to individual manufacturers, and freight charges to the stores or distribution centers are costs included in the price you pay. Add to these hidden expenses the local delivery charges, or the shipping from the factory to your home directly, and you can see that freight is a major expense. This is particularly true for furniture, since freight charges are based on bulk. Therefore, if you can pick up a purchase directly from the manufacturer, or just save the cost of local delivery, you will realize quite a savings.

Many bulky pieces arrive with damages. This is frustrating but not too serious. A minor damage or a slight scratch can easily be repaired; besides, it will happen sooner or later under normal use. If you inspect everything that you buy with a magnifying glass and insist that a minute blemish is cause for returning what you have bought, you will find the procedure extremely difficult and often totally frustrating. Since upholstery, special finishes, choices of colors, and so on, often involve handwork, you must also count on human error. However, it may happen that what you have carefully selected and ordered arrives with major damage or in the wrong fabric; in that case you must insist that the piece be exchanged. It is surprising how often mistakes occur, and it is sad how often dealers try to avoid their responsibilities to the buying public. Knowing these facts—perhaps anticipating the worst—should prepare you to face the furnishing of a home with equanimity.

On that note, this guide comes to a close. Whether in large or small choices, it is my hope that you will enjoy your creative efforts at design. I hope, too, that I have made clear throughout this book that there are no absolute rules about anything in design. Don't feel pressured by what books, magazines, or other people tell you. Try to follow some of the suggestions, or all, only if they make sense to you. Don't become compulsive about the many aspects of design. If you approach the design of your home in a relaxed way, based on some knowledge and prior planning, you should have lots of fun. And if some of the suggestions contained in these pages help you to do so for small cost, or even for less money than you thought you would spend, you should have achieved good design on a budget.

INDEX